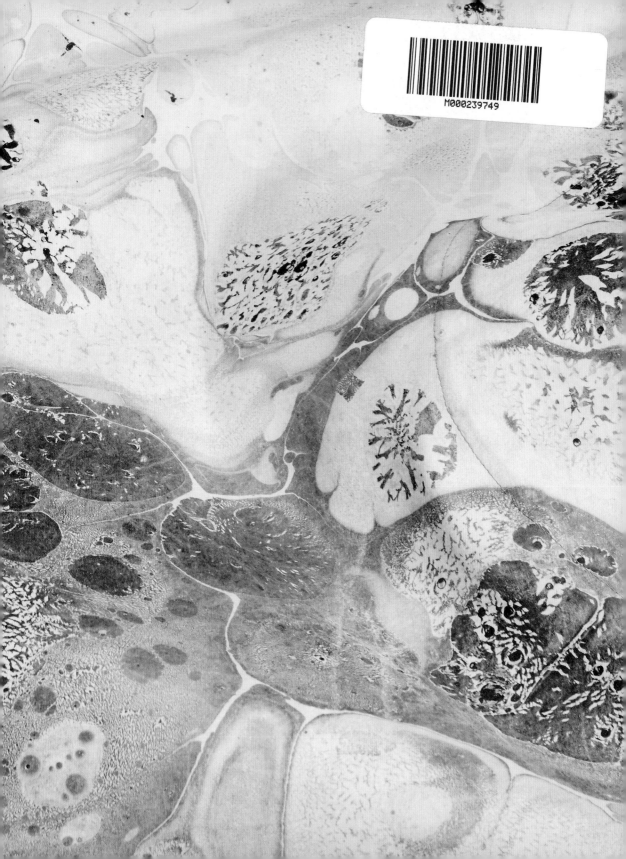

Toronto Makes

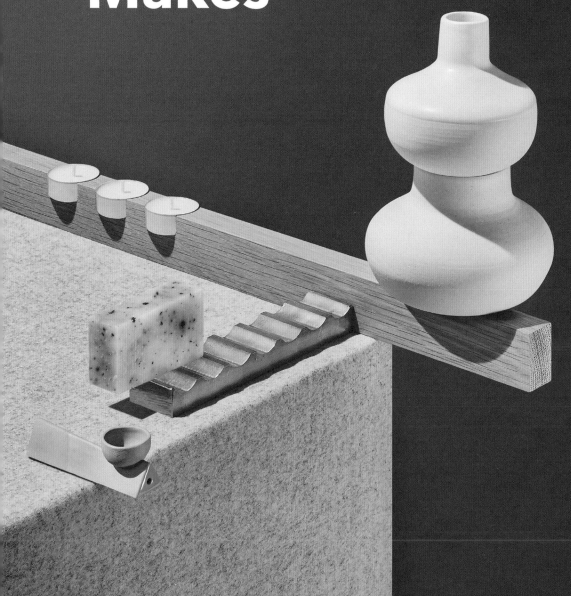

Toronto Makes

the things we love
and the people
who make them.

Randi Bergman

Figure.1

Vancouver / Berkeley

For my makers
(a.k.a. my mom and dad)

FRONTISPIECE: Rekindle oak tealight holder, Mima Ceramics vases, FILO TIMO brass object, Matter Company biodegradable soap, High Noon stoneware pipe

OVERLEAF: Tasso Baking croissant, Mima Ceramics cup, Rekindle oak plate, Kroft ash side table, Talia Silva porcelain bottle, Anony wall sconce, Dean Davidson gold and brass collar, High Noon stoneware pipe

FACING: CXBO chocolate egg, Michelle Ross bronze bracelet, Contrabotanic wool felt succulent, Rekindle oak plate, 18 Waits Japanese-cotton tie, High Noon stoneware pipe, ATTIC gold bangle and ring

Contents

Introduction

As an equal opportunity consumer who loves the high, low, and everything in between, and as a creative entrepreneur in my own right, I was
honoured to help give voice to those who put their blood, sweat, and
tears into creating timeless, beautiful products. Their shared perse-
verance became a constant source of inspiration while writing this
book. Getting to know each maker and illuminating the unfailingly
complex stories behind their brands was instructive to the creator
in me—there are over fifty routes to creative fulfillment represented
through the stories in this book, and none of them are simple. The steps
are all here though, if you're willing to follow them.

Randi Bergman

We love a backstory. We love finding out why and how makers, entrepreneurs, and business owners create the things we covet. This curiosity is how we arrived here, to *Toronto Makes*. It's been a joy to discover our local makers and peruse their wares—textiles, libations, eats, furniture, objects, art, and indulgences. This collection of makers represents the quality goods this city offers. They make Toronto a little more special, a little more interesting.

The brands and products made in our city, make our city. We hope the next time you crave a coffee, gift a pair of earrings, need a bar of soap, hunt for swim trunks or a new shirt, or search for a side table—whatever it may be—you go out of your way to find the goods with a story. And we hope your search ends in Toronto. Incredibly, it's all here.

Amy Czettisch

MAKEJOY

Est. 2008   # 18 Waits

"I always knew I wanted to create a lifestyle brand," says Daniel Torjman. "It's not just about selling shirts—it's about telling a story." And he should know—routinely layered in tailored button-downs underneath an artfully perched fedora, the designer embodies his line of rugged menswear staples, 18 Waits.

The Ottawa native grew up camping, listening to Bob Dylan, and studying the outfits of those around him. "Fashion aside, things that were styled nicely or designed in a great way interested me from a very young age," he says. His fascination eventually led him to New York, where he studied fashion merchandising management at the Fashion Institute of Technology while interning and then working for Rogan Gregory, a pioneer of selvage denim and eco-friendly wares.

In 2008, Torjman relocated to Toronto, where he launched 18 Waits as an ode to another of his troubadour heroes, Tom Waits. "The inspiration behind the whole brand is very much a rock 'n' roll lifestyle, particularly of the seventies," he says. At the outset, the line consisted of custom fit graphic T-shirts and sterling silver jewellery, which Torjman peddled around town in a rumpled duffel bag. The line was an instant hit with retailers, and soon grew to include everything from waxed outerwear to printed scarves to timeless three-piece suits. "We'll never make anything that you'd find in the back of your closet in ten years and think, 'What was I thinking?'" Recently, Torjman expanded into the world of miniatures with Hopper Hunter, a line of kids' clothing named after his son and designed to match the brand's adult styles.

Each 18 Waits piece is designed at the brand's studio and produced locally, using fabrics from Canada, the U.S., Japan, and Portugal. "The two pillars of 18 Waits are attention to detail and high quality," he says. "I feel that in order to maintain control of both we need to be able to know our factories, to be able to go there and visit the people who are running it all."

Today, Torjman's vision is best expressed through his Queen Street West flagship, which carries his own designs alongside LAFCO candles and accoutrements and jewellery by LHN and Misc. Goods Co., all surrounded by vintage décor. The brand's studio operates from just behind the shop, allowing shoppers face time with the team. "You don't have to go somewhere else in the world when you can find people doing good things in your own backyard," he says. "We're a small team but everyone really cares. It makes all the difference."

PRODUCT
The Dylan Shirt, The Signature Tie

MATERIALS
100% Japanese cotton   Slim-fit button-down and tie

3

My Le Nguyen (left) | Co-founder, Vice-President
Rock Huynh | Co-founder, President

Est. 2013 1925 Workbench

One of the most exhilarating hallmarks of the maker movement is that something as age-old as a barn door is up for exploration. What's been around for centuries isn't just good enough as-is—it's fodder for something new, improved, and completely innovative. Case in point, the ingenious work of the husband-and-wife team behind 1925 Workbench.

Rock Huynh and My Le Nguyen met in karate class as teenagers after the two immigrated to Canada from Vietnam. As a young married couple, Huynh worked in IT and Nguyen as a registered nurse, but when they bought their first home—a tiny, 800-square-foot fixer-upper—they discovered their calling. "We built a powder room at the back of the house, and we couldn't have a swing door because it would have been in the way," says Nguyen. Huynh built a barn door instead, which re-awakened his passion for making. "Back in Vietnam, Rock lived near a carpentry shop and he'd watch the carpenters every day. He was fascinated. I think he has a natural inclination towards making things, and once given the opportunity, it just exploded." Shortly thereafter, the couple launched 1925 Workbench as a side-project to make custom furniture and hardware. Within a few months, it was their full-time gig.

While they offer a range of furniture, wooden barn doors with hardware are the company's signatures. "They're special because they're

"A maker's mind is always moving, solving problems as they're making." **My Le Nguyen**

so functional," says Nguyen. That, and they're surprisingly versatile—from a pink Edwardian door with solid brass hardware to a black door featuring a curved corner window, they offer endless possibilities. The couple has also patented single-track bypass hardware, which allows for two doors to bypass on one track instead of the usual two. Their brass, steel, and hot-rolled metal offerings are a more streamlined take on traditional hardware.

In an age of mass production, Huynh and Nguyen are particularly passionate about the local maker movement and local sourcing—their wood is all from Ontario, while metals are milled in Quebec. "It's extremely important for us that we have the business in Canada and things are being made here," says Nguyen. "It's important that we slow down and make things from our own hands."

PRODUCT
Single-Track Bypass Hardware
(Patent CA2964538)

MATERIALS
Brass

Two doors that bypass on one
track (also available in raw steel
or stainless steel)

Anony

When god said, "Let there be light," s/he surely meant good lighting design, right? Cue Anony, an interdisciplinary studio bringing together function and organic form through innovative, thoughtful design.

Launched in 2015 by Christian Lo and David Ryan, Anony is an antithesis to the ornate, overly fussy chandeliers of decades past. "We like to create designs that are timeless," says Lo. Timeless, sure, but with an impact—case in point, its standout Dawn light, made of a trio of Plexiglas circles draped over a suspended aluminum tube, which resembles the changing horizon at sunrise.

Lo and Ryan studied at OCAD University and Humber College respectively and met while working for another lighting company. "We work really well together as a team and we started thinking about how we could create lights with our own aesthetic and design values," says Lo. Working with new technologies and locally sourced materials whenever possible, the duo focuses on modular LED lighting that dazzles customers and critics alike. What's more, they keep price points within reach. "Because lighting can have that artistic 'wow' factor, pricing can get a little arbitrary," says Lo. "We like to keep it honest by keeping prices at a point that customers can understand based on materials, labour, and design."

"A light has two lives:
when it's lit, and when
it's not." **Christian Lo**

The Dawn light is perhaps the most overt example, but Anony's
entire collection is an ode to the designers' environment. "Dave and I
really like to start with what we have here, what our skills and manufacturing capabilities are locally," says Lo. The two also opt for accessible and easily recyclable materials. "A lot of lighting designers like
to fuse things together, but then you can't disassemble those pieces
to replace a part, or even recycle it. You have to throw the entire fix-
ture out," says Ryan. "Designing products that can be disassembled is
really important to us, and we're using materials that can be recycled
so if something breaks down or something happens, the part doesn't go
to a landfill."

Sticking to their guns on these points meant that Anony's first
five-piece collection took over a year to make, debuting in 2017 with
the Ohm, an opal glass orb with interchangeable shells, and Horizon,
a wall sconce that mimics a floating ring of light. "We have a hands-
on approach with prototyping," says Lo. "We don't like to go straight
to production—we want to make sure we create a good quality product
that is really well thought-out."

PRODUCT
Ohm Floor Lamp

MATERIALS
Steel, aluminum, glass, LED

Suspended lamp weighted by steel base and illuminated
by opal glass spheres with polished brass shades

David Ryan (left), **Christian Lo** | Partners   11

Melissa Gobeil (left),
Susan Shaw | Co-founders

Est. 2015   # Attic

Leonardo da Vinci once said that simplicity was the ultimate sophistication. Or was it Gwyneth Paltrow? In any case, it's a sentiment true enough to be the foundation of many businesses in this book, especially ATTIC, a line of elegantly unencumbered fine jewellery launched by two best friends in 2015.

Melissa Gobeil and Susan Shaw met nearly a decade ago in goldsmithing school. "As fate would have it, we sat down right beside each other," says Shaw. The two grew close and began fantasizing about their own line. "We were doing a lot of scheming and dreaming and creating an alternate future reality we wanted to build together," says Gobeil. After they graduated and tucked a few years of custom jewellery experience under their belts, they launched ATTIC on the premise of creating simple, lasting pieces, which were seemingly hard to find at the time. "We heard over and over that people were having difficulty finding beautiful, everyday pieces," says Shaw. "It felt like the right time to jump in."

The duo splits duties; Shaw spearheads design in their Toronto studio, and Gobeil manages business and marketing from her home in Guelph. "When we come together in the studio a few days a week, it's magic," says Gobeil.

Working with locally sourced, recycled, and new gold, the duo distills classic jewellery styles into their simplest forms. "We draw from

"When we first met, we were on a mission to go into business. We wanted to work in this creative field and make a living at it. That was very much a part of the story of ATTIC from the beginning."

Melissa Gobeil

shapes that have been around forever, like the signet ring or a gold hoop, but refresh them with a more modern character," says Shaw. That character is epitomized with their use of grey diamonds and untreated Montana sapphires, which adorn rings with a natural, soft pigmentation. "Most sapphires are heat treated, so that the colour is intensified," says Gobeil. "What we're using is the gemstone in its natural state—no two stones are alike."

As with most fine jewellery, a good portion of ATTIC's work is in engagement rings and reworking heirloom pieces, in which case the pair use both old and new techniques, such as 3-D modeling and hand carving wax. "It's a technical field and there are a lot of design problems we're solving all the time, but when it boils down to it, we're thinking about how our pieces feel on a person and how that's going to carry them forward in their lives and into the next generation," says Gobeil. "What's going to make it interesting and beautiful enough that you can wear it when you're eighty?"

PRODUCT
Clockwise from top: *Plateau Ring,*
Marquise Diamond Torc Ring, Archer Ring

MATERIALS
Diamonds,
14K yellow gold

Cast-gold rings from
the Union Collection

PRODUCT
Bather Surf Trunk

MATERIALS
100% polyester

A tailored surf trunk with
an above-the-knee cut

Est. 2013   # Bather

Putting aside the improbability of a swimwear brand thriving in the Great White North, there's still plenty to be surprised and delighted about when it comes to Bather Trunk Company. Kyle Kaminsky founded the brand in 2013 after he struck out while trying to find a swimsuit on vacation in Croatia. "I went to the beach in a suit I'd had for ten years and I realized, 'This is unacceptable!' So I bought one that was super expensive, super uncomfortable, and gave me a rash," he says. He was still on the hunt when he got home—and quickly learned that there was no such thing as a well-made, well-priced men's suit.

So, with little sales know-how and zero design experience, Kaminsky prototyped a single style and manufactured it in three colourways. His favourite retailers scooped up the entire run. "It was unbelievable that they would give somebody who knew nothing about anything at the time an opportunity," he says. His instincts were on point, though—the retailers sold out.

Kaminsky ramped up Bather while subsidizing growth with funds from his nine-to-five at a family business. The side hustle became his full-time gig a few years later. "I quit a job I was probably supposed to have my whole life. It was scary, but whatever. That's life, right?"

"At the end of the day, nothing's getting made without the initial steps of me grabbing a pair of scissors and cutting up some fabric and tie-dyeing it in my bathtub."

Today, Bather is a twice-yearly beachwear line based around two core styles: the surf trunk (a fitted board short) and a looser, mid-thigh-length swim trunk. Each style features prints designed by Kaminsky and his brother Evan, an art director. "We're inspired by anything from architecture to interior design, but there are always little nuances to our styles." Take, for instance, a recent Hawaiian print, which appears sunny from afar but depicts a bloody shark attack close up.

Despite its oft-tropical prints, Bather has been decidedly rooted in Canada from the outset. All design, drafting, and prototyping is handled in-house, and production happens at a nearby factory in order to keep overhead low, but still local. For Kaminsky this is both a financial and a personal decision. "If you're having goods made cheaply overseas, you're crossing your fingers and hoping everything's going alright. I can drive to my factory and see what's going on any day of the week," he says.

Kyle Kaminsky | Founder   19

PAPER TIGER

5.3% ABV

DRY HOPPED
PILSNER

500 ML

BELLWOODS
BREWERY

BREWED & BOTTLED IN TORONTO / 124 OSSINGTON AVE

CHERRY
MOG

FEBRUARY 2018 · 5.9% ALC./VOL. · 500ML

WILD ALE
FERMENTED
ON FRUIT

BELLWOODS
BREWERY

BREWED & BOTTLED IN TORONTO / 124 OSSINGTON AVE

BARN OWL

SOUR ALE WITH RASPBERRIES AND CRANBERRIES
BARREL AGED 18 MONTHS

NO.13

BELLWOODS BREWERY

BREWED & BOTTLED IN TORONTO / 124 OSSINGTON AVE

PRODUCT
Paper Tiger, Cherry Mog, Barn Owl

MATERIALS
Craft beer

Dry hopped pilsner; wild ale fermented on fruit; barrel-aged sour ale with raspberries and cranberries

Bellwoods Brewery

Est. 2012

Given the abundance of craft beers now livening up shelves across the city, it's hard to imagine that just a few years ago our options were limited to "domestic or imported." This seismic shift is due to innovators like Mike Clark and Luke Pestl, two academics-turned-brewers who opened the boundary-pushing Bellwoods Brewery on the trendy Ossington strip in 2012.

Hot on the heels of the craft brewing movement south of the border, Clark and Pestl opened Bellwoods to offer an alternative to the mass-produced beers that saturated Toronto at the time. "We were having to drive to Buffalo to find beer that excited us," says Pestl. "There weren't very many IPAs, hop-focused, or sour beers offered in Ontario, which all added up to us opening up shop." Alongside a small group of breweries, Bellwoods paved the way for quirky, experimental flavours like its Jelly King (a hoppy sour) and Jutsu (an aromatic pale ale) to be considered a new norm. Since opening, Bellwoods has opened a second brewery and bottle shop, while the number of craft breweries in the province has exploded to over 250, forty-four of which are in Toronto.

Bellwoods sells most of its beers directly from the Ossington outpost, allowing for a whole lot of creativity. "We don't necessarily design fresh beers to be shelf-stable. We're more concerned with having the

"We built a business from the brewery out as opposed to coming at it from the other end—a businessman can hire a brewmaster, but it won't be the same." **Luke Pestl**

best aroma and taste possible, which sometimes goes contrary to practices that would ensure a good shelf life," says Pestl. "We have a high rotation of brews. We are constantly trying something new." Case in point, a fruity lactose pale ale made in collaboration with Evil Twin, a Brooklyn-based brewery. "It's a riff off the first collaboration we made together, but updated with different fruit and with lactose sugar, which adds to its creaminess—it's about as experimental as it gets," says Pestl.

"We've grown a lot in the last few years but not as much as we could have, to be honest," says Clark. "We want to work with the team we have to make the company as sustainable as possible and the products as consistently good as possible." Which means pouring out brews that don't pass muster. "It's always quality over quantity. We're not afraid to dump things down the drain that would probably be perceived as fine but just aren't up to our standards. There's a lot of integrity in that."

Mike Clark (left), **Luke Pestl** | Co-founders   23

Corrine Anestopoulos | Founder,
Creative Director

Est. 2004 # Biko

Corrine Anestopoulos has been making jewellery since the eighties. A self-professed crafty kid, she'd invent her own friendship bracelet styles and gift them to her appreciative pals. "I prided myself on coming up with new and unique things for them," she says. "They loved it!" By the time she made it to Ryerson University's new media program, that old passion had knocked again. "I put a pair of earrings on for a friend's fashion photography project and just loved the way the photos came out. I thought, 'I feel like a new me,'" she says. She started tinkering with her own beaded styles at home and in 2004 began selling them as Biko, a line named after her childhood nickname. "I couldn't believe it. People were eager to pay for something I'd made for fun! It seemed too good to be true," she says.

Since those early days, Biko has morphed into a continually evolving collection of "modern nostalgic" earrings, necklaces, bracelets, and rings. "I love the hunt for inspiration. For today's modern aesthetic, I use a mix of materials, sleek metals, fluid forms, and textures that complement, contradict, and play off one another," she says. As for many, travel is the key to unlocking her creativity; Anestopoulos counts recent trips to Greece, Australia, and Mexico among her greatest design inspirations. "I love looking at architecture and the lines on

PRODUCT
Solarwave Studs

MATERIALS
14K gold- or rhodium-plated brass

Sculptural twisted studs with hypoallergenic
posts (available in three sizes)

buildings and shapes and reworking those ideas into a lot of the pieces," she says.

Biko is currently in over 150 stores worldwide, but despite the high volume, each piece is still handmade locally, a process that is carefully overseen by the designer herself. Anestopoulos frequently uses vintage materials, which she sources from nearby manufacturing hubs that were dominant before the wave of offshore mass production. The materials for her deadstock tortoiseshell pieces, for example, are from the U.S. east coast, the former hub of costume jewellery. "I love sourcing unique hard-to-find materials and incorporating them alongside my own hand-poured castings, giving each piece my own modern twist," she says. What's more, Anestopoulos's team includes workers from the formerly thriving local jewellery industry.

Today, Anestopoulos is having just as much fun as when she started. "It's a joy working with magical little objects and finessing their design until the piece is just perfect," she says.

"Through local events and showing my work around Toronto, I've built friendships and relationships with people and have become part of a community. It's something I didn't see coming and it's something I love."

PRODUCT
Onedge Rocker

MATERIALS
Birch plywood, stainless
steel hardware

A cantilevered rocker
made to flex for comfort

Brothers
Dressler

Est. 2003

Some might say that Jason and Lars Dressler tower over the Toronto
design scene, and not just because they're both six-foot-eight. The
brothers have transformed some of the buzziest spots into veritable
nature scenes—from the beloved pergola that enwraps the dining space
of Drake One Fifty to an undulating, sixteen-foot solid-oak bench at the
J W Marriott in Muskoka. "I like to think that rather than approaching
some of our pieces as architects, we approach them as gardeners, working the materials with our chosen methods and allowing them to grow
into something new," says Lars. Using only responsibly sourced, sal-
vaged woods and metals, their imaginative designs have helped shift
the mindset about the possibilities in reclaimed materials.

As teens growing up in Malton, Ontario, the brothers balanced bud-
ding basketball careers with a shared fascination for reworking wood
and found objects into skateboard ramps. "We were always seeing what
we could make out of what we could find in our parents' garage," says
Lars. They both initially pursued engineering, but a few years into their
respective careers became frustrated by how far away they were from
the hands-on work. Jason enrolled in the craft and design course at
Sheridan College, where a few of his furniture pieces caught the eye of
the design world. That was enough of a spark for them to set up shop,

"Being a maker is about allowing yourself to work with your hands—and creating something original out of materials that, to some people, might be diamonds in the rough." **Lars Dressler**

which they did in 2003, sharing a single bench. Those early pieces (notably, the Onedge lounge chair) remain part of the company's repertoire, which has grown to include both small-batch and one-of-a-kind furniture and lighting.

A naturalistic, Scandinavian current runs through the brothers' work, which could be attributed to the various woods they source from Ontario forests and through local waste streams. "A tree has so much potential and the city is disposing of hundreds of thousands of trees a year," says Lars. They've begun sourcing metals in this way too— "rather than just sending them to the scrap, there's so much energy and engineering put into those objects already so we try to figure out a way we can incorporate it into the design, even if it's a subtle way where it's not really seen or noticed." To wit, their Branches chandelier features an automotive piston in its hardware. "We're often looking for something that pushes us to come up with new ways to make things," says Lars. "Sometimes we can't help ourselves but create something that doesn't exist."

Lars Dressler (left), **Jason Dressler** | Principals   33

PRODUCT
Felt Succulents

MATERIALS
Merino wool, terracotta

Succulents and
cacti created with
needle-felting

Est. 2014

Contrabotanic

For those of us who have a particularly lethal history with succulents, Contrabotanic is just the fix. Amanda Perumal's life-like felted versions are not only delightful, but they solve the existential dread of millennials who lack the generationally prescribed green thumb. "I killed all the succulents and cacti I bought for my home," she says.

Perumal was studying textiles at OCAD University when she came across felting, a technique for wool manipulation. "One of my final projects was a felted terrarium and the idea of that was really interesting to my classmates," she says. They encouraged her to make smaller versions that could be sold, and a few months later she enrolled in Summer Company, an Ontario-funded program for students starting new businesses. There, with the help of mentors and business advisors, Contrabotanic was born. "It wasn't something I thought I'd continue with after those three months, but it just kept rolling," she says. Perumal's creations became a hit across the city at markets like One of a Kind and Etsy: Made in Canada, where she was voted most popular vendor.

Perumal felts each piece with needle in hand, and with live plants surrounding her for inspiration. Because of the nature of the technique, pieces rarely look anything other than one-of-a-kind. "Most of

"People appreciate the time
and effort that goes into
making them by hand.
The process adds value
and not many people are
familiar with it."

the plants I've made are based on plants I've actually owned, which helped me out in getting a more realistic form," she says. Perumal has been praised for the refinement of her pieces, each of which can take upwards of six hours to make.

Perumal's eye for clever interiors extends to her full-time job working with a decorative arts team at an interior design firm, where she draws on her interest in Japanese and Scandinavian interiors. "I admire both interior design styles for their humbleness and appreciation for natural material, so I'm slowly trying to collect pieces and objects to surround myself with," she says. To that end, she hopes to expand Contrabotanic with a line of custom ceramics as well.

Coolican & Company

Est. 2015

What's so cool about Coolican & Company (pardon the pun) isn't just that its quietly elegant furniture is catching eyes around the world. It's that despite the international attention, its founder, Peter Coolican, remains a distinctly local signifier of the possibilities coming out of our fair town.

Like so many makers, Coolican's initial studies (in economics and urban studies) are what inspired him to pivot from the world of desk jobs. "I started getting lost in the architecture library, which is where I discovered people like [famed mid-century designer] George Nakashima, who were making a living off furniture that wasn't stock—they were fusing handmade with design and that really appealed to me," he says. After graduating from McGill, Coolican went to Rosewood Studio, a world-renowned woodworking school in Perth, Ontario, to spend six months training before moving back to Toronto to open his own studio.

At first, he was making complicated custom pieces and barely turning a profit. "It didn't inspire me," he says. So he took some time off, regrouped, and wrote a business plan for what is now Coolican & Company, centred on small-batch furniture that's built to stick around.

"I want to make stuff that's going to last, both aesthetically and physically," he says. "It has to be stuff that'll fit into multiple aesthetic

PRODUCT
Edwin Chair in Blackened Oak

MATERIALS
White oak

A contemporary take on
the classic Windsor chair

spaces, which usually dictates something simple, contemporary, but with a traditional feel." Durability may be of the utmost importance to Coolican, but it doesn't oppress his quiet design sense. Take, for instance, the waif-legged Palmerston stool, or the elegant, arched Euclid mirror, which inspires a sense of calm.

Each batch consists of around twenty pieces made with locally sourced white oak, which Coolican says "allows us to keep the quality really high, prices accessible, and to be able to manage the quantity of parts so that they're still handmade but made efficiently." The company works in collaboration with the Ministry of Natural Resources to ensure the promotion of Ontario wood. "People probably aren't aware that Ontario, especially the Niagara region, has some of the most fertile soil and some of the most beautiful wood," he says.

Alongside Nathan Clarke (director of craft and production) and Stephen Dalrymple (director of creative development), Coolican designs each piece through a combination of hand sketches and full-scale model work. "We spend a lot of time together going over things. Especially through that prototyping phase, I'll be back and forth with those guys a lot," he says. "The 'and Company' thing is very real to us."

"Sustainability comes down to making something that's not going to be thrown away. If we're going to pull those resources from the ground, we want to use them well."

Ryan Tavares (left),
Jay Mitchell | Co-founders

Coup
de Tête

Est. 2014

In the lexicon of rock 'n' roll, there are few style markers as essential as a well-worn hat. Whether a droopy wide brim à la Joplin or a crisp Bowie-inspired fedora, the head-turner is back in a big way thanks to Coup de Tête, a bespoke hat label firmly rooted in the old school.

"We're using timeless techniques and fusing them with a modern sensibility, which I think is what being a maker is all about," says the brand's founder, Jay Mitchell. "We like to call it 'burning tradition.'"

Mitchell fell in love with hat making while working in a hat shop on his time off from touring with his own rock band. "I used to customize all the hats I'd get from the store," he says. "I'd pull out the brims, add my own flair to it, and that started being what people would come in for." All the attention got him fired, so he decided to start his own line out of his apartment. Through Mitchell's music connects he was able to create tour pieces for high-profile members of July Talk, Gorillaz, and Sloan, which set Coup de Tête in motion. A few years later, he partnered with Ryan Tavares, a leathersmith with equal penchant for torching convention.

The duo now works out of a studio hidden on Dundas West near the Ossington strip, handcrafting and hand-stitching their hats from start to finish, while experimenting with unorthodox techniques like

> "We're the guys you come
> to when you can't quite
> find what you're looking for."
> **Jay Mitchell**

carving, tattooing, or burning holes with an open flame. The results include everything from a powder-blue fedora with a carved, golden patina, to one embellished with feathers and a vintage king of hearts playing card. While each piece is a keepsake, it's also an amalgam of relics in and of itself: "Our felts come from Tennessee, but we have family and friends all over the country grabbing treasure for us to embellish our hats with," says Mitchell. "Whenever my fiancée throws away a dress, I'll cut off the bottom foot of it to use. I'll trim the dress and hem it, and then we'll donate it."

The duo's magpie approach means each hat is impossible to replicate. "I love giving a guarantee that this hat is for you and no one will ever have it but you. It's a blessing and a curse," says Mitchell. "It's why people love what we do but it's also why I have yards of random fabrics strewn across the studio."

PRODUCT
Custom Wide-Brim Hat

MATERIALS
100X beaver felt, vintage fabric,
leather, eagle feather, coin

A handcrafted hat with a 4-inch
brim and teardrop pinch

Coyote Flowers

The journey towards makerdom is sometimes circuitous and full of false starts. Other times it's simple, as in the case of Lauren Sellen, a floral designer who found her métier in the most obvious place. "I had a long list of potential career options after studying performance art, and my sister said, 'You've always had an interest in flowers. Why don't you try that?'" she says. "My first reaction was, 'Doesn't everybody?' I didn't think it was unique to me."

Turns out it was. Because the Winnipeg native's interest in flowers isn't just about creating beautiful bouquets: it's about transforming natural objects into works of art. "I love the idea of flowers as sculpture and using them in unusual ways," she says. She decided to jump in, and after a few years of honing her skills under other floral designers in Toronto, in 2016 she founded Coyote Flowers, a studio dedicated to the ephemeral nature of, well, nature. "When you think about it, flowers are these crazy living things with so many tiny well-designed parts. They move, change, and then change again—they never stay the same."

Sellen's background in performance art lends a bit of drama to her arrangements, which often blend rare buds like lady slipper orchids ("they're like slippers for a fairy") alongside the once-mundane likes of baby's breath to create unusual shapes and moods. "I'm surrounded by

"I feel like I've always had in me this need to create."

buckets of flowers, I have my music on and I really try to shut out everything else," she says of her process. "I'm really not satisfied until I feel like it effortlessly communicates a feeling."

Coyote Flowers is part of a new wave of unconventional floral studios rising thanks to the online resurfacing of traditional art forms. "I think people are always drawn to natural elements, but it was an area that became stagnant," she says. Nowadays, experimental florals have become the calling cards for disruptive young megabrands like Glossier, who Sellen recently collaborated with. "I think we're all pushing each other to see where it can go. It's really exciting," she says. "Most floral designers, from all over, are all so supportive of each other because of Instagram. It's the coolest industry. Everybody is friendly with each other and is inspired by each other. It's this weird new community of artists."

MATERIALS
Uva stalks, orchids

A sculptural hanging installation
made of organic material

Lauren Sellen | Founder, Creative Director   51

PRODUCT
CXBO Signature Collection

MATERIALS
Chocolate

The original nine
bonbon flavours in
a hand-painted box

CXBO
Chocolates

Est. 2015

"When I was a kid, I watched *Willy Wonka & the Chocolate Factory* and it was a revelation to me. I've wanted my own chocolate factory ever since then," says CXBO founder, Brandon Olsen. Olsen is, arguably, Toronto's Willy Wonka. His technicolour treats are just as fantastical as the ones in the famed tale but one better: they're real.

Before his ascent to chocolatey glory, Olsen was a prodigious chef who started in the kitchen at age fifteen and worked his way up to an apprenticeship at The French Laundry in Napa Valley, where he first witnessed the inner workings of confectionery. "I loved watching the chocolatiers at work, so I bought every book and watched every video I could find to learn how to do it myself," he says.

Back in Toronto, he rose to head chef at The Black Hoof and Bar Isabel, two of Toronto's most notable eateries, before ultimately leaving to chase those Wonka dreams. "After Brandon quit Bar Isabel, he started making these amazing splattered chocolates and they really struck a chord in me," says his partner, Sarah Keenlyside. They were a hit on social media, too, and Olsen was flooded with requests. Keenlyside, a former arts and video producer who's now CXBO's creative director, urged Olsen to move forward with his artistic approach. The pair officially set up shop in 2015 in Kensington Market.

"The mark of a maker is not only making things with your hands or technology, but also with your heart."

Sarah Keenlyside

CXBO's chocolates and bonbons are still handmade in the Baldwin Street space; the chocolate is imported from France and then melted, tempered, and poured into polycarbonate, hexagonal moulds. Each mould is hand-painted with coloured cacao butter beforehand, which gives it the vibrant, Pollock-esque signature. Bonbons are filled with caramel ganache, a sumptuous glaze filling. Olsen's pièce de résistance is the Ziggy Stardust Disco Egg, a psychedelic wonder that you have to smash—if you can bear it—to uncover the treasures inside. The confection has quickly become a Toronto icon.

CXBO is a labour of love for Olsen and Keenlyside, who focus on production and design respectively alongside a small but mighty team. "Brandon has an extremely refined palate and a real aptitude for making food that requires specialized processes or scientific thinking," says Keenlyside. "My whole world leading up to starting CXBO concerned aesthetics. Together we make a really great team. Especially with chocolate, which is so sculptural—it lends itself to an artistic approach."

Brandon Olsen | Owner, Founding Chocolatier
Sarah Keenlyside | Owner, Creative Director

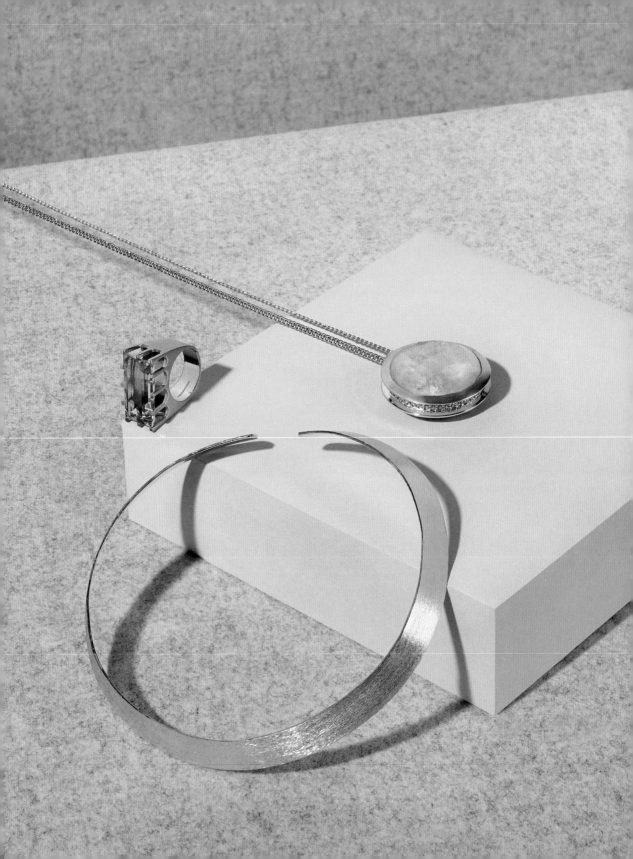

PRODUCT
Castle Ring, Essential Collar,
Coliseum Pendant

MATERIALS
22K gold-plated brass,
semiprecious gemstones

Sleek, minimalist
pieces made with
artisanal methods

Dean Davidson

Est. 2007

Dean Davidson always thought he'd be a veterinarian. Growing up in small-town Manitoba, he was surrounded by fields, farms, and plenty of cattle. "The fashion world was so foreign to me," he says. In 2002, while working as an agronomist in Calgary, he took a trip to South Africa that would forever change his course. "I bought a bracelet at a market in Cape Town," he says. "I was out with friends back home one night and they said, 'Somebody should make those.'" Inspired, Davidson bought all the supplies and immediately got to crafting. The bracelets were so good that he decided to approach a local store, which promptly snapped them up. Shortly after, he moved onto fashioning cuffs from vintage leather belts, which scored him an opportunity to create jewellery for designer Paul Hardy. The two collaborated for three years, before Davidson moved to Toronto to launch his own line.

In 2007, utilizing the silversmith training he'd picked up from the Alberta College of Art + Design, Davidson launched a collection of bracelets, necklaces, and earrings made with beads and hand-brushed metal, a technique he had learned in Paris. "I'd sit for hours, brushing metal to achieve the perfect finish," he says. With a few collections under his belt, he'd learn to simplify, opting to cast his sculptural designs using 3-D modeling.

"I feel like I was fortunate to have worked in a different career prior to this. It taught me a great deal and, in some ways, led me down the path to become the designer I am today."

Over a decade later, the brushed finish is a signature of his five-plus yearly collections, which are stocked in over 250 high-end retailers worldwide. Each piece is made of brass and plated in 22-karat gold or rhodium, which is then inset with a variety of semiprecious gemstones such as black onyx and labradorite. Davidson, who cites travel as a frequent form of inspiration, sources a wide range of hand-cut and hand-polished jewels from Jaipur, India, where the collection is produced in a family-owned workshop.

"They are wearable and versatile pieces but also something you've never seen before," says Davidson. "The line has an artisan feel to it." Despite the fact that the business has expanded dramatically, Davidson still honours his maker roots. "I think every designer starts out as a maker," he says. "I started making every single piece myself but grew that into a designer business. That's the definition for me. I'll still sit there and make pieces with my hands—my company has just grown to the point where I need more people to facilitate it."

Dean Davidson | Owner, Creative Director   59

Alexa Schoorl (left),
Mariel Gonzalez | Owners, Designers

Eleven Thirty

Est. 2013

A decade after the designer bag mania of the 2000s, it seems that discerning customers have fallen for a very different sort of investment piece, one that's refreshingly logo-free and built to last—enter Eleven Thirty. The leather brand has earned a cult following for sophisticated, understated bags, which are handmade in Toronto by its two founders, Mariel Gonzalez and Alexa Schoorl. "Whatever's the opposite of trendy, that's what we are," says Schoorl. "We're never looking at what's in style when we're designing. It's more about what will be in style for a long time."

A classic design sense has been central to the brand since its early days in 2010, when Gonzalez, a Ryerson School of Fashion grad, launched her own leather brand fresh out of school. A few years later, the self-taught Schoorl joined her as a studio mate. The two hit it off and decided to join forces. "We were like, 'How are we going to share space without copying each other? We should just do this together!'" says Gonzalez. Five years after they started, the partners describe their bags as an equal blend of their respective aesthetics and personalities. "Eleven Thirty is literally just Mariel and me mashed together, but I don't think there's any part of it that's specifically one or the other," says Schoorl. "We design each bag together and throw the design back and

"Sometimes I think when
you're a maker, it's just in you."
Alexa Schoorl

"It's like a weird compulsion."
Mariel Gonzalez

forth until it's perfect." To ensure the highest quality, the duo works with local suppliers of Italian leather. "We don't throw away any scraps, so any leftovers get made into other pieces," says Schoorl.

Usually the duo spends about a week perfecting a style, though some, they say, take years. "We have a few bags, like the Katie and the Anni, that we launched right away, but over the years they've evolved as we've learned more about our customer and gotten more solid in our aesthetic and quality," says Gonzalez. "We're guided by what the brand has shown us it is, and at its best, it's mothers and daughters buying the same bags."

PRODUCT
Romy Tote in Salt and Pepper

MATERIALS
Leather, brass

A classic tote with handles
and shoulder straps

F. Miller Skincare

Est. 2014

There's a lot to be said for radical simplicity, the ethos behind Fran Miller's sophisticated line of active botanical skin care oils. Beloved equally for its elegance and effectiveness, Miller's arsenal has amassed a loyal clientele, popping up on the shelves and the feeds of the most stylish beauty buffs. "Without losing any of the important values of the product itself, I think we take an artful approach," she says.

After years of struggling with her own skin sensitivities, Miller began to experiment with mixing oils she purchased at a health food store. Using oil on your face was a relatively new concept at the time, scarcely mentioned in the skin care market. "There's always been a misconception about oils, that people with acne-prone skin shouldn't use them," she says. "To my surprise, they worked so much more effectively than what my doctors had prescribed me."

After more experiments and research, F. MILLER launched in 2014 with a single product: a multipurpose face oil composed of over fifteen botanical oils and herbal extracts. "The goal was to minimize the skin care routine and help it be as effortless as possible," she says. To wit, extracts such as tamanu oil for scarring, neroli for oil reduction, and evening primrose for anti-aging work in tandem to pack a singular, streamlined punch. Slowly, Miller expanded into body oil, hair oil, and

PRODUCT
Clockwise from top left: *Hair Oil, Cleansing Oil, Beard Oil, Shave Oil, Toning Mist, Body Oil, Shave Oil, Face Oil*

MATERIALS
Botanical oils, plant extracts

Skin care oils and essentials made from natural botanical ingredients

67

a range of tightly targeted products for each body part. "The beauty of oils is that they're so multifunctional," she says.

As a self-described "product whore," Miller finds inspiration in everything from art to architecture to food. Her unique perspective is also informed by her background in the fashion industry; she graduated from Ryerson School of Fashion and worked in retail management and wholesale before launching her brand.

Miller's intuition has proved invaluable. In the five years since her launch, facial oils have become *de rigueur* in the natural skin care industry. The newcomers are scarcely as aesthetically pleasing as Miller's bottles, though, which gleam with the kind of minimalism Phoebe Philo built.

Miller sees her products at the intersection of green beauty and high design. "For me, it's about combining my minimalist aesthetic with a potent product," she says.

"We're pushing an effortless routine that comes down to daily rituals and essentials. In a way, we're simplifying lives that can be very *not* simple."

PRODUCT
Cappellacci d'Anatra and
Cappellacci ai Funghi (zig-zag
edges), *Tortelloni di Ricotta*

MATERIALS
Eggs, flour, buckwheat,
spinach, duck, porcini
mushrooms, ricotta cheese

Famiglia Baldassarre

Est. 2010

The world of Famiglia Baldassarre is a magical place, dotted with duck-filled cappellacci, ravioli di ricotta, and other fresh, handmade pastas that are at the heart of many of Toronto's most beloved eateries.

Leandro Baldassarre is something of a wunderkind in the local food scene. He grew up in the kitchen, where his grandmothers would frequently hold court. "We come from pretty poor Italian roots, so food is the glue that holds the family together," he says. At age eighteen, while attending Humber College's culinary program, he made a fortuitous connection with noted Toronto chef David Lee, who hired him to work in the kitchen of Splendido, a local institution at the time. Baldassarre soon dropped out of school and worked every station in Lee's kitchen, before deciding to set off for Italy in pursuit of the many shades of the region's cuisine. "To see how adherent and in love they are with their own culture in different towns, and how rooted that was in the history of that specific area, is very eye-opening," he says. While there he worked at the Michelin-starred Dal Pescatore in Mantua, a region known for rich, vegetable-forward dishes.

Baldassarre returned to Toronto in 2010 and started making traditional pasta fresca by hand in a College Street basement owned by Lee (Baldassarre's first client was Lee's popular eatery Nota Bene). Word spread, and Baldassarre's creations soon became citywide favourites.

"If I were to open a restaurant I think it would take away the magic of what is here. We can cook whatever we want, when we want, and enjoy it purely."

Famiglia Baldassarre's over twenty-five pasta varieties—like its tagliatelle, which are individually cut from a sheet of velvety, golden dough—are all made using traditional methods and imported Italian flour. "Any time I'm thinking of making a pasta, I start from the top down," says Baldassarre. "I think, 'What was my best experience eating this pasta?' I can remember a place in Emilia-Romagna or Parma where I had that tagliatelle with butter that was the best I ever had—I think of texture, colour, flavour, and start working backwards." His journeys towards cavatelli and tortelloni are similarly romantic.

Famiglia Baldassarre supplies over forty local businesses out of its Geary Street kitchen, which began serving its own mouthwatering menu of dishes for local patrons in 2017 on an exploratory, limited basis. "Giving people visual access to what we're doing—you can sit here and have lunch and watch our production—goes full circle," he says. There are a few staples, such as tagliatelle with butter and Parmigiano-Reggiano, but mostly, it's a self-professed toss-up of seasonal dishes, such as pumpkin ravioli in autumn and spaghettoni with mint and zucchini during the summer months. "You're cooking five feet away from people waiting for their plate. They eat it and tell you how great it was or how it reminded them of something. And that's the moment of pure satisfaction. It makes everything else great. Even if you've had a bad day, it can make the day great."

PRODUCT
Elements of Design

MATERIALS
Bronze, brass, nickel, steel

Process pieces from
the workshop floor

Filo Timo

Est. 2015

Aristotle was pretty quotable, and one of his best aphorisms must be "The whole is greater than the sum of its parts." It explains a lot about FILO TIMO, a fine architectural metalwork studio dreaming up bespoke components. "We're translators," says Erica Pecoskie, who founded the company alongside her partner, George Simionopoulos, in 2015. "We listen to every nuance of our clients' hopes for the project. We go from thought to action to object, without losing any of that richness in the process."

After both working as architects, the two came up with the idea for the studio after creating a model time machine (yes, you read that right) for a particularly eccentric client. The *Doctor Who*–inspired sculpture featured everything from vintage monitors to light modulators fashioned from leather, bronze, and stone. "It was like jewellery at the scale of architecture," says Simionopoulos.

FILO TIMO has crafted pieces in a range of size and complexity, from custom signage to a heliport, all of which gleam with their signature opulent flair. While most of their work is kept under wraps to respect the privacy of their clients, some of the duo's favourite pieces are currently on public display across the city in signage that's strikingly creative—and, says Pecoskie, collaborative. "We're really

"We fabricate the way our forefathers did, and our granddaughters might."

Erica Pecoskie

energized by the imaginations of our clients," she says. "We take that dream in one hand, and make it real with the other." Take, for instance, a baguette they recast in bronze for the door handle of Forno Cultura bakery on King Street. "We did it for a laugh, but it turned out well!" says Pecoskie. "We had Andrea bake a few options, which we then brought to the foundry to cast in bronze. It's marvellous to think of the molten metal picking up every detail of the original."

The notion of making is baked into the philosophy of FILO TIMO, which is from a Greek expression meaning "the love of making." "It's the passion you place in an object that you've made that then carries that embodied care," says Simionopoulos. To make those objects the duo uses many techniques, including 3-D printing, laser jetting, and water jetting. "We have a bit of a preoccupation with not wasting materials," Pecoskie says. "If we use a sheet of bronze or brass, which are both valuable, some might say luxurious, we optimize their use. I suppose our answer to the challenge of sustainability is to make high-performance products that last."

Erica Pecoskie | Partner, CEO
George Simionopoulos | Partner, Chief Design Officer

Est. 2013 # Fitzy

Perhaps one of the most unifying factors among makers is the circu-itous route they travel to finding their craft. For Fitzy designer Robin Fitzsimons, it took post-grad disillusionment, Tumblr, and reclaiming a whole lot of creative freedom for her to arrive at her now-thriving line of leather accessories.

"At OCAD I developed a very focused and thoughtful way of making, where every single aesthetic decision needed to be justified," she says. "It led me to create some great pieces of art, and do a lot of overthink-ing." So, after a year working at a custom art studio and a year studying psych at the University of Toronto, she started a 365 project, during which she made something creative every day for a year. "I started drawing, painting, making jewellery, and posting it all online," she says. "The response was really positive, and people kept suggesting that I sell what I was making. I just figured . . . why not?" So she launched an Etsy page to do just that, starting off with leather jewellery and eventually pivoting to the streamlined wallets, purses, and backpacks that would soon become her signature.

Fitzsimons describes her aesthetic as clean, minimal, and util-itarian. "I always try to keep my pieces really simple, with an eye for how they'll actually be used," she says. Each piece usually begins with

"I love buying stuff that's made in Canada because you're supporting the Canadian economy but you're also supporting our craft culture."

digitally sourced inspiration and a series of sketches. "It's kind of this big collage process where you take elements from a hundred different things and combine them all together into something completely different and new," says the designer. She frequently includes her customers in the process too, using social media to mine for their preferences—they've voted on everything from closures to colourways. "I'm always trying to find the right balance between what I think looks and works really well, and what the customers want," she says.

That the end product usually resembles something modern and slick is a testament to Fitzsimons's craftsmanship, considering that everything is made by hand using solid brass hardware and locally sourced leathers. "For me the most important thing isn't that an item is handmade but that it's ethically made," she says. "Usually, buying local, small business, handmade items means you know that your money is going towards the person who made that thing and that they're getting paid a fair wage and making something that's beautiful and will last a long time."

PRODUCT
*All In Wallet, Mini Wallet,
Monogrammed Key Fob*

MATERIALS
Vegetable-tanned
leather, brass

A trio of minimalist
essentials

Glory Hole Doughnuts

Est. 2012

Some origin stories take you on a journey through mind, body, and soul. Others are as simple as, "I just really love making yeast products!" That's the case for Ashley Jacot De Boinod, founder of Glory Hole Doughnuts, a Parkdale bakeshop that has been a cult favourite since opening back in 2012. The appeal is obvious: what's better than a treat that's glazed, frosted, or filled? Where Glory Hole sets itself apart is with its from-scratch approach to the fluffy stuff—each doughnut goes through a sixteen-hour transformation, from mixing to fermentation, before reaching your lips. "We start before the sun comes up," says Jacot De Boinod. "Everything is made in-house with high-quality ingredients using very little machinery, which has always been important to me."

While not limited to the yeast variety (the shop makes cake and vegan doughnuts as well), Jacot De Boinod prefers them. "It's especially difficult being a maker that uses yeast because it's such a transformative, organic ingredient," she says. "At the same time, I've always loved working with challenging ingredients."

It's easy to believe she loves a challenge—before launching Glory Hole, Jacot De Boinod shape-shifted around various Toronto kitchens, from Buca to Live Organic Food Bar. The diverse approaches she

"I have the utmost respect for anyone making doughnuts. It's not the easiest thing. Anyone doing it is a friend of mine."

learned prepared her to narrow her focus. "I remember in chef school having a theory class centred around artisans. I grew fascinated with how one person could spend their entire career creating and perfecting one thing really well. There's a lot of honour in that," she says. "I always knew I wanted to do that: one thing really well."

And that she does. A sampling of Glory Hole's menu is enough to make even the sugar averse quiver with desire. Just picture it: olive oil–glazed lemon ricotta cake-style doughnuts, Earl Grey–glazed doughnuts, or ones modelled after the ol' cash register staple, Ferrero Rocher... it's almost too much. "A lot of my inspiration comes from years of trying things out in the kitchen," she says. "I like doing classic or iconic desserts like birthday or Black Forest cake, and turning them into doughnuts." And while Glory Hole is known for its innovative flavours, Jacot De Boinod thinks of herself as a traditionalist. "My favourite doughnut is Toast and Butter," she says. "It'll always be on the menu."

Ashley Jacot De Boinod | Doughnut Mistress

PRODUCT
Clockwise from top left: *Latte Crunch, Milk and Cookies, Ferrero Rocher, Toast and Butter, Pecan Crunch*

MATERIALS
Yeast-raised dough

A selection of yeast-raised doughnuts from the winter 2018 collection

HANDMADE
est. 2013

Grinning Face

NON-DAIRY GELATO GOODNESS

16 oz

MADAGASCAR BOURBON VANILLA
VANILLE BOURBON DE MADAGASCAR

HANDMADE
est. 2013

Grinning Face

NON-DAIRY GELATO GOODNESS

16 oz

DARK AND HANDSOME CHOCOLATE
CHOCOLAT NOIR RAFFINÉ

PRODUCT
Madagascar Bourbon Vanilla (top),
Dark and Handsome Chocolate

MATERIALS
Handmade coconut milk

Artisanal gelato made from
fresh coconuts

Grinning Face

Est. 2013

For most, food allergies represent a world of limitations. But for Keo Phokeo-Williamson, they led to opportunity. The former industrial designer was on mat leave, spending time with her son. She, her husband, and her son are all lactose intolerant, but "it was summer and we wanted ice cream," she says. The craving led her to taste test a variety of dairy-free brands, all leaving her unsatisfied. "Something was always missing," she says. "The ingredients were artificial, the texture and flavour were off, it was all wrong."

So she started making her own at home using the Thai coconut milk she grew up loving. After a year of perfecting it, Phokeo-Williamson's recipe was so good that her sister, Julie Phokeo, joined in. With Phokeo's training as a pastry chef, "we knew right away we'd make a great team," she says. The duo launched Grinning Face Gelato in 2014.

"In the beginning, we'd crack all the coconuts, make the milk ourselves. We worked tirelessly, doing everything by hand," she says. Nowadays the labour is divided—Phokeo-Williamson handles the sales and business side and Phokeo is in charge of production at their West End facility—but the sisters still make the milk themselves, united by their inherited passion for good food. "When my parents came to Canada they didn't understand North American food culture," says

"My son loves our gelato and tells people about it. He's really proud. It's nice to feel like you're making a product with integrity."

Keo Phokeo-Williamson

Phokeo-Williamson. "In Thailand, mass-produced food wasn't so prevalent. They made everything from scratch, including coconut milk, and passed their love of food on to us."

Grinning Face is renowned for its ultra-creamy gelato, which is the result of its artisanal approach. Local, seasonal ingredients like rhubarb, berries, beets, and stone fruits are churned separately into batches of coconut milk, which have each been crafted from scratch. "We make each coconut milk with different fat profiles to create a different mouth feel for certain flavours," says Phokeo-Williamson. "It's a lot of work but produces much better results." Their inventiveness results in flavours like Wild Blueberry and Hawaiian Basil, or Sweet Corn and Roasted Pineapple. "We don't use artificial additives," she says. "You can't hide flavour."

Despite beginning in a small walk-down shop on Parliament, Phokeo-Williamson hopes that Grinning Face is one day the stuff of big business. "Today, food culture in Canada is in a much better place," she says. "People are more conscious—they care about what goes into their food, how it's made and where. We want to be part of that revolution."

Julie Phokeo (left) | Co-founder, Chief Operations Officer
Keo Phokeo-Williamson | Founder, Chief Creative Officer

(Left to right)
Odin Cappello | Design Director
Rod Fitzsimmons Frey | Founder
Savi Pannu | Creative Director

Guild
Eyewear

Est. 2013

Given the proliferation of eccentric eyewear currently on the market, one could assume that it was a relatively new trend. Fashion-forward frames, however, date back as early as the 1930s, a time Rod Fitzsimmons Frey harks back to with his bespoke frame brand, Guild Eyewear. "The styles that women were wearing back in the thirties, forties, and fifties are so incredibly wild," he says. "As manufacturing technology becomes more accessible, small companies like ours are able to make exciting, experimental frames at a more accessible price point using modern methods."

Those modern methods are what inspired Fitzsimmons Frey, a computer engineer turned software entrepreneur, to create Guild in 2013 when he relocated to Toronto after launching a series of tech companies in California. "I wanted to start something that was more about working with my hands and creating nice things for people, rather than electrons and bits and bytes on a screen," he says.

That, and he has a larger than average head. "I've always had trouble finding glasses that fit me, and as I started talking to people about various products that they wished had more variety, eyewear came up time and time again," he says. And so, Guild Eyewear's "guided bespoke" experience was born: The brand works with clients to create custom

"I believe in using modern technology to make locally manufactured goods economical for a larger audience, not just the 0.1 percent."

frames with the right shape, colour, and fit. "We can customize everything from where the bridge sits to the subtlety of the frame shape," says Fitzsimmons Frey.

The brand creates ready-made frames as well, finding inspiration in bespectacled rock stars (Jarvis Cocker) and octogenarians (Iris Apfel) alike. Each pair is made at Guild's West End studio using Mazzucchelli cellulose acetate (a sturdy mix of cotton and wood fibres), and takes ten days to shape, sand, and polish in a computer-automated milling machine before being assembled by hand.

While bringing high-quality eyewear to a broader range of clientele is the goal, Guild will remain an intentionally small company, according to Fitzsimmons Frey, who currently works alongside his creative director, Savi Pannu, and design director, Odin Cappello. "One of the core principles I have is that there is a sort of person out there who wants to know the makers of the products they're buying and they want to have a relationship with that object," he says. "That's the sort of person I want to serve because I'm one of them and I would like to provide those people with high-quality things. You can't do that unless you're there."

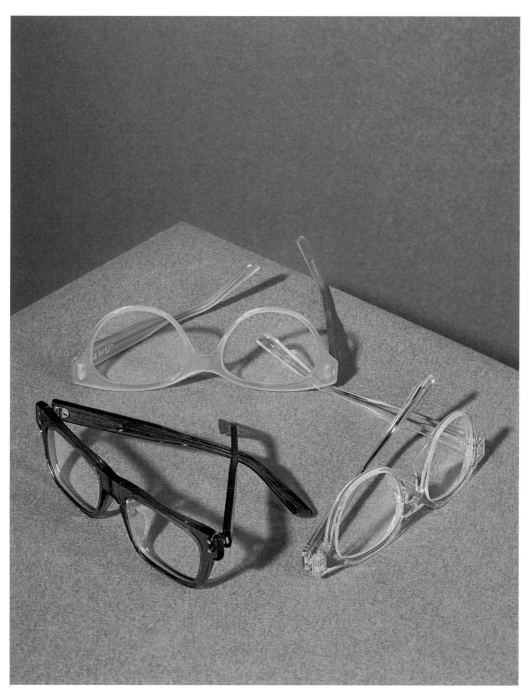

PRODUCT
Frames from the Guild Collection

MATERIALS
Mazzucchelli cellulose acetate

Handmade, vintage-
inspired eyewear

Heidi Earnshaw Design

Est. 2000

The world of small-batch woodworking may be experiencing a renaissance, but the spectacularly graceful work of Heidi Earnshaw has quietly been making formative marks on the Toronto scene for almost two decades. "My work is certainly based on a traditional language, but made more contemporary by paring back and relying mostly on small details to give the piece character," she says.

Earnshaw got her start in the sculpture studio at the University of Toronto, where she first explored woodworking as part of a fine art degree. "My teachers often accused me of making work that was too 'functional' or furniture-like," she says. It wasn't until she began crafting small furniture pieces such as coat hooks and blanket boxes as a means of making money post-graduation that she saw it as a career. "At that point I understood that I didn't want to make art, I wanted to make functional things," she says. She began seeking out woodworkers and blacksmiths, and ultimately moved into a West End building inhabited by a bunch of Sheridan College craft and design graduates who inspired her to enroll in their former program. She did, while simultaneously founding her business, in 2000.

Earnshaw is now old-hand at creating work that is elegant and unassuming, but, like the chests and drawers she's so beloved for, reveals its

"You need to respect the material. Wood is a natural, living material. It fluctuates with the seasons and will continue to do that for the lifetime of the piece of furniture."

depths upon closer inspection. "Light and shadow, careful proportions and the materiality of the wood itself—it's a kind of quiet aesthetic that unfolds over time through the intimacy of use and allows the work to become a backdrop for our daily lives."

Earnshaw's work sits in some prestigious institutions, like Aga Khan Park in north Toronto and Canada House in London. While this might seem like laurels enough to rest on, Earnshaw sees these pieces as collaborative works of art. "Each piece is an experience for both the client and me as a maker, rather than just a consumption," she says. This folds into Earnshaw's environmental approach, which is similarly reflected in her use of exclusively North American wood. "While there are beautiful woods coming from other parts of the world, many of those systems of deforestation aren't very well regulated," she says. "We have lots of beautiful wood that's grown right here."

Earnshaw is one of the best heritage-quality designer/makers we've got, but she's uncomfortable with reverence. "I feel like I've got another twenty years to go before I can call myself a master craftsman," she says. "This is a long and deep journey into really understanding the material and all that is possible with it."

PRODUCT
Butler Sideboard

MATERIALS
Carrara marble, quarter-sawn white oak

Traditional joinery and solid wood throughout

Heidi Earnshaw | Designer, Maker   97

Heidi McKenzie

Est. 2012

It's safe to say that Heidi McKenzie is a woman of many talents. In previous lives, she was a math and science prodigy, a classically trained pianist, a radio producer, and an arts fundraiser. "I was that kid who got scholarships everywhere and had no idea what I wanted to do with my life," she says. All of that changed at the age of forty, however, when her parents downsized and gave her some of her childhood things. "My mom handed me something I'd written when I was nine years old saying I wanted to be a potter when I grew up," she says. "It was like a lightning bolt went through me—I'd forgotten how in love I was with the idea of turning earth into objects."

Just like that, McKenzie was on a plane to her father's ancestral home of India to apprentice alongside a master ceramicist who had been a childhood friend of her husband's. And there, in a small town abutted by the Himalayan Mountains, she learned to make her own clay and to wheel-throw at rapid speed. "I was working and throwing ten hours a day, six days a week. It was amazing," she says. Upon her return, she completed a diploma at Sheridan College, an MFA at OCAD, and several international residencies in Australia, Indonesia, and beyond.

A residency in Jingdezhen, China, led to McKenzie's first solo show, *China Unbound*. The show featured a series of sliced, patterned porcelain vessels meant to "reflect the dualities and tensions of the country."

"Even my pots...they're
not just pots, they're an
expression of a story I have
inside of me."

From there, she mounted *Clay in Motion*, an exhibition at the Canadian
Clay and Glass Gallery in Waterloo, which featured her earlier works
Anima, curled-up bands of thrown "faux metal" clay that nod to her bat-
tle out of fibromyalgia; and *Maru*, a series of interlinked rings meant
to symbolize community. In 2017, McKenzie changed direction with
Spaces Within, an Oz-inspired series of hand-built coiled stoneware
and terracotta pieces that grew out of her experience working with
Aboriginal artists in Australia's Northern Territory.

McKenzie describes much of her work as abstract portraiture,
which allows her to reflect on a wide range of cultures and conditions
in a "non-figurative, abstract, minimalist art that everyone can relate
to." McKenzie's process is equally fluid, oscillating between hand-built
sculpture and the slipcast or wheel-thrown functional wares currently
sold at ceramic shops worldwide. "My work is really disparate, but I like
the variety," she says. "Lots of potters have a signature look and they're
making that ten hours a day for twenty years. I'm not that person. I like
to switch things up constantly."

PRODUCT
Whimsy

MATERIALS
Grogged stoneware and porcelain slips

Hand-coiled abstract sculpture,
fired in gas kiln, 32 × 19 × 14 cm

PRODUCT
Clockwise from top: *10 After 6*
in speckle, *High Noon* in white,
8 AM in grey

MATERIALS
Stoneware clay, glaze

Hand-built sculptural pipes

Est. 2017

High Noon

"Now that it's finally legal, I think it'll become so normalized that having a pipe within the same line as dinnerware will no longer seem
strange," says Leah Lavergne. The cannabis ceramicist grew up staying
away from pot for fear of its effects on her competitive dancing career.
Fast-forward a decade, and the Ottawa native is spinning a newfound
appreciation of the herb into her line of aesthetically pleasing pipes,
High Noon.

   "When I moved to Toronto, I was meeting more and more people who
were in the cannabis industry and thought very differently of the plant,
which shifted my perspective," she says. Lavergne began toking—and
shopping around for stylish vessels to suit her new favourite pastime.
"I found a piece I really loved in a local shop, but then quickly realized
it wasn't a locally made piece, which kind of turned me off," she says.
"I wondered why I was paying so much for something that wasn't
made in Toronto."

   Serendipitously, Lavergne had just enrolled in classes at The Shop, a
community ceramics workshop and studio. She was soon able to create
her perfect piece and so, right there in a plume of smoke, High Noon
was born. "I really wanted something to smoke through that I was
proud of and I was happy to have around sitting on my bedside table

"With so many great things
coming from Toronto,
I just want to be building
where we are."

or coffee table," she says. Lavergne played around on the pottery wheel before she switched to casting and perfected her method: each pipe is cast in three parts using a plaster mould. "Everything is done sandwich style," she says, which allows for the air tube to be formed inside each piece before it's finished by hand.

Lavergne has become known for a minimal, feminine aesthetic, which she says is a reference to both her dance background and her friends. "I love to create organic shapes with a little movement in them, but there's also a rigidity to them, which I've always attached to the more technical parts of dance," she says. "I'm really inspired by the women in my life." It seems that inspiration is flowing right back.

Leah Lavergne | Designer, Maker   105

Hinkleville
Handmade

Est. 2015

Sure, light therapy and vitamin D are more commonly prescribed to cure a case of the SADs, but have you ever tried adorable pottery? Enter the sunny world of Hinkleville Handmade, a line of ceramic *objets* dreamed up by Janet Hinkle in 2015. "Vibrant colours and fun shapes always tend to catch the eye, but it's the faces that seem to make people really happy," she says of the smiley little creatures that inhabit Hinkleville. It's fitting, given that the line was a way out of an unsatisfying desk job for Hinkle, a fine arts grad. "My friend gifted me a pottery wheel and I was looking for something to do with my hands," she says. "The next thing I knew, it totally snowballed into a new career."

Currently, Hinkle is producing up to 750 pieces per month. And while the influx of business is a dream for most makers, its realities often lead to the kind of stress that can break a burgeoning business. "I think the biggest struggle, at least for a lot of makers I've talked to, is managing stress," she says. "I tell makers who are newer to it than I am, 'You're doing a great job but if you realize you're getting stressed out about certain things, be on top of it.' You don't realize how serious the physical and mental effects of stress can be over time."

Hinkle's story is similar to many others in the gig economy. "It can be difficult to find a steady job, and so people are trying to create

"I've never been somebody who uses a sketchbook. I just start with a lump of clay and see where it goes."

opportunities on their own," she says. "Trying out the maker world is perfect [for that] and we now have all these different maker spaces opening up around the city, which has made it more accessible."

Hinkle's referring specifically to Akin Collective, the West End studio she works out of alongside artists, designers, illustrators, and ceramicists. "I've been lucky to have found a studio with a wide range of mediums, where everyone is really supportive," she says. "If I wanted to bounce an idea off a silk screener, she's right there. You get a different take on your work than a ceramicist might give you."

Much of Hinkle's work is light and airy in hue. "I am often inspired by Nordic design and the colours, shapes, and patterns of mid-century design," she says. Her penchant for pastels is also a product of the high-fire clay she most regularly moulds with. "I like it because it's durable, but one day I'd love to master low-fire clay, which allows you to achieve fluorescents and brights," she says. "I love to look through fashion magazines for colour palettes and explore what's possible to recreate with pottery supplies."

Janet Hinkle | Founder, Principal Designer

PRODUCT
Moon Mug

MATERIALS
Stoneware clay, glaze

Made with locally sourced clay and food-safe glaze, with a wax-resist cut-out feature

109

PRODUCT
*Bolt Sconce, Squaretown
Stool, Oldtown Stool*

MATERIALS
Walnut, white oak

A solid-walnut LED sconce
and asymmetrical hand-spun
solid-oak stools

Hollis + Morris

Est. 2014

If the remarkable rise of Hollis + Morris could be used as a case study for the resonance of Canadian design, we'd all be sitting pretty. "Three years ago, I was doing this out of my garage," says founder Mischa Couvrette. Today his distinctive, minimalist pieces sit in the offices of global giants like Nobu, Google, and Facebook.

Couvrette launched Hollis + Morris at the International Design Show in 2014, with seven products based around the idea of well-crafted furniture and lighting that is timeless, functional, and versatile. Over the years, his output hasn't slowed—Couvrette and his team design five to eight new products every year, each with customizable sizes, configurations, and finishes. Their recent Lantern Pendant, for instance, is made from a customizable wood and LED channel that can take form in an endless combination of shapes.

Couvrette studied marine biology at Dalhousie University (Hollis + Morris is named for a Halifax intersection he lived near), where he was exposed to architecture through a roommate. "I was fascinated by the projects he was working on and I took a liking to helping him out." After graduation, Couvrette and a few friends refurbished an aging steel sailboat before cruising it from Halifax to Guatemala. "It needed a new engine, new interior, new floors, new sails . . . basically new everything,"

"There's an ignorant optimism that I keep pushing forward to make this thing bigger. I enjoy taking risks. I live on that edge."

he says. Safely back in Toronto, Couvrette enrolled at Sheridan College, where he honed his skills before launching Hollis + Morris. "Because there are no frills on a sailboat, it lent itself to the minimalist aesthetic I ended up creating as a brand."

Recently, the brand opened a 2,400-square-foot showroom in the same building as its manufacturing facility in the city's West End, increasing its total space to 9,000 square feet. Most everything is made in-house, save for a few details, like its recent foray into metal spinning; firms elsewhere in Ontario helped with the production of an aluminum basin table.

"Something I really love about the design process is that it is never really finished," he says. Couvrette attributes much of the brand's success to versatility, though its clever designs certainly add to a mass appeal. "Each piece seems to take on a life of its own by adding a new material or placing it in a new space. I think versatility is just as important as function."

Mischa Couvrette | Founder, Designer   113

Hunt and Gather

Est. 2017

"Dark and edgy" isn't a descriptor frequently attached to wedding florals, but Tellie Hunt is most comfortable off the beaten path. "I knew from the beginning that I wanted my brand to be a little different from most flower shops," she says of Hunt and Gather, the studio she launched in 2017. The moody, taxidermy-filled High Park spot feels just as boudoir as it does botanical. "I take a lot of my inspiration from Dutch master paintings and old English gardens."

Flowers have been a part of Hunt's life ever since she naively applied for a floral designer position at a Newmarket shop at age fourteen. She was hired despite her lack of experience, and came up the ranks by assisting with small bouquets and trimmings before a brief stint pursuing a career in tattoo art. "I knew I needed to be creative to make a living, so I decided to give flowers another go," she says. Hunt began freelancing at floral shops across Toronto, learning different techniques before opening a space all her own. "I like to describe my design style as unstructured arrangements that reflect nature and the way the seasons change . . . the tones of the leaves, the early spring flowering branches."

Hunt's blooms are mostly sourced locally, which she says allows for greater experimentation. "I tend to get a lot of leeway with my clients

PRODUCT
Large-scale Centrepiece

MATERIALS
Foxglove, garden roses, companula, ranunculus, mock orange, lisianthus, peonies, chocolate cosmos, eremurus, heuchera, begonia, tweedia

117

in terms of what blooms we use as we send their colour palettes to the farmers and receive mixed buckets directly from the fields," she says. Among her local favourites are *Fritillaria* for spring, foxgloves for summer, and *Nicotiana* for fall.

Hunt develops customized arrangements largely for weddings, which she says bring her the most joy. "It's a pretty special thing to be involved in one of the biggest days of someone's life," she says. The works are often created in collaboration with her clients, as well as planners and photographers. "I am always surrounded by creatives who make visions come to life. Whether it is planning a perfectly curated event or baking a cake that is a piece of art, it is a very strong, creative, and inspiring community."

"I truly value finding out about diverse cultures and marital traditions. I feel like this is something pretty special about working in such a wonderful, multicultural city."

Jess Hotson Textiles

Est. 2015

While some makers see their craft as an escape from an increasingly digital existence, others thrive by oscillating between the two realms. Take, for instance, Jess Hotson, a graphic designer and creative director who in her spare time uses 100 percent real wool to weave winsome tapestry art. "I've always been in the arts, painting, drawing, and messing around—which is what originally led me to graphic design—but I'd never found another medium I loved until I came across textile art," she says. "So much of my time is spent on the computer that it's nice to have that thing on the weekends that's about as far away from technology as you can get: playing with wool and rope."

Hotson came across woven tapestries while digging online for inspiration for her own home. "It started with me really wanting to buy one," she says. "It was so interesting to see such a resurgence of old, celebrated textile arts from the sixties and seventies." She reached out to notable Brooklyn-based weaver Maryanne Moodie, who sold her a starter kit and a loom of her own, made of wood, which was rare at the time. Hotson experimented by creating small pieces for friends. "I became a bit obsessed with perfecting it," she says. This eventually led her to the Haystack Mountain School of Crafts, a retreat for makers in Maine. "It was interesting to go through this process after I'd already

"It's super meditative to just stand in front of this thing, thinking about nothing but that thing, for hours... There's a repetitive motion that clears your head."

taught myself, learning techniques that really excelled my practice," she says. "I was there with weavers I'd been following on Instagram for years who are full-time, amazing artists. It really validated my love for it—being surrounded by other people who are passionate."

Long gone are those newbie days, though. Demand for Hotson's pieces is now so high that she's mostly stopped taking custom orders. "Two Christmases ago, I was churning out so many commissions that the product began to suffer," she says. "At this point, I only take ones that are special to me or will teach me something new about my craft." And sure, she's able to be selective because her weaving is secondary to her full-time job. "I think my work is getting better because it does have that individual love and care going into it," she says.

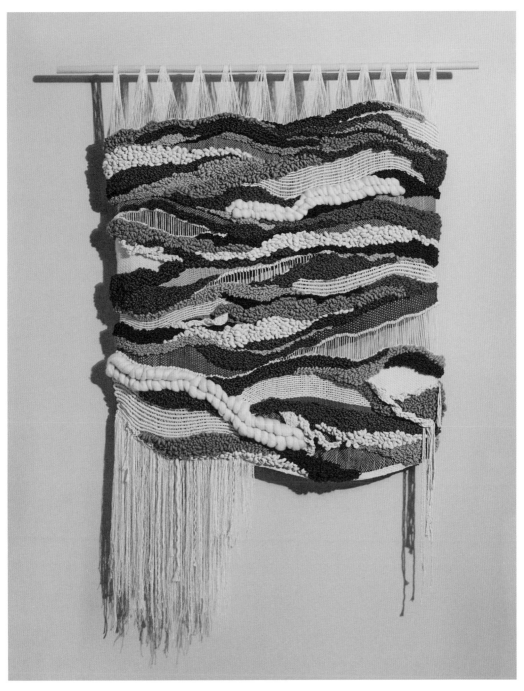

PRODUCT
Woven Wall Hanging

MATERIALS
Wool, rope

Made from woven, knotted,
and braided wool and rope

PRODUCT
Buoy Floating Nightstand

MATERIALS
Solid wood

A minimalist nightstand
with a drawer that runs on
soft-close slides

Kroft

Est. 2015

Sure, skill is essential to a successful career. But any go-getter would agree that a bit of blind faith goes a long way, too. It was in the mix for Dustin Kroft, who left a booming self-built business to dive into the uncertain waters of furniture design and manufacturing. "I prefer not to describe it as a calling, but I had this blind comfort of knowing I would find a way to make it work," he says.

Kroft has always been a dreamer. At age nineteen he founded a successful moving company that would grow to a team of sixty in just five years. "Just as the business started to do really well, it dawned on me that I was maybe not doing what I should be doing," he says. He began dabbling in vintage furniture dealing on the side, which led to a night course in woodworking. So, he sold his first business and took a year to immerse himself in the furniture industry, while heeding cautionary tales about its great many challenges. But entrepreneurial experience was something Kroft had plenty of, and soon he debuted his eponymous line of accessible, mid-century inspired furniture at the Interior Design Show in 2016, to much fanfare.

Kroft's first collection featured linoleum-accented credenzas and dressers, all designed with high function in mind. Its wall-mounted

"I think aesthetically it's about using as many natural materials as we can and building them in a way that shows them off."

Buoy floating nightstand, which came a year later and is still a standout to this day, features plenty of storage. "We want to really dial in on how people interact with the items," he says.

While function is a pillar of the brand, much of its pared-back aesthetic derives from the natural materials it uses. Kroft sources only from local lumberyards, citing walnut, oak, and ash as woods intrinsic to his modern designs. "I really do believe that half of what makes anything beautiful is how it's made. There's a heavy focus on craftsmanship here. We're supreme wood nerds!"

Dustin Kroft | Founder, Lead Designer   127

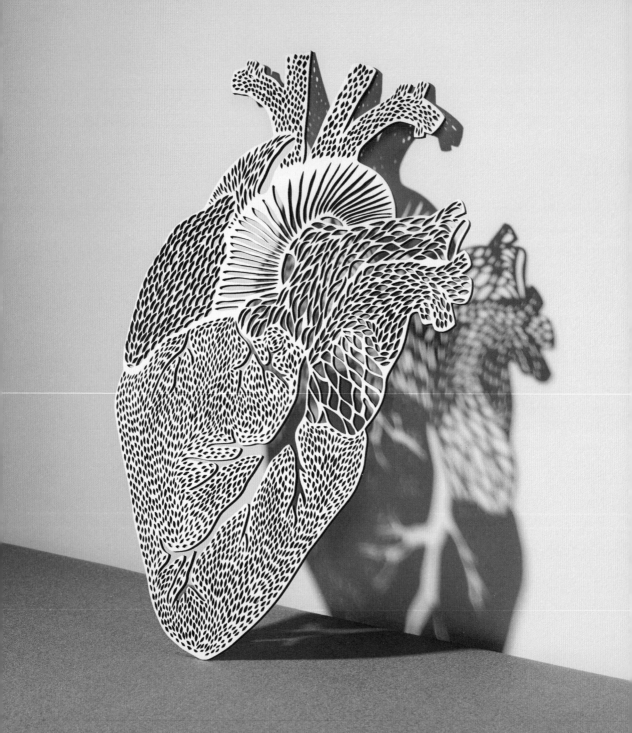

PRODUCT
Anatomical Heart

MATERIALS
Birch wood

Wooden laser-cut
wall art, 40.6 × 25.4 × 0.3 cm

Light + Paper

EST. 2012

Ali Harrison's unlikely journey towards makerdom is a shot to the arm for anyone who's ever been less than thrilled with their formative artistic leanings. "I was never praised for my drawing or painting skills," she says. "Nobody would have ever said, 'She's destined to become an artist.'" But over a few years, with the help of a box cutter and a kitchen cutting board, Harrison found her calling.

Harrison had been researching DIY Christmas present ideas when she came across papercutting, an art form whose origins date back nearly two thousand years to the Han dynasty. She tried her hand at the ancient craft, creating a heart shape for her aunt. She may have destroyed her tools in the process, but pretty soon Harrison was hooked. When she wasn't working in the dean's office at the University of Toronto she was honing her new skills. "I'd go home every night and spend six hours making paper cuttings," she says. Meanwhile, she purchased a laser-cutting machine, which she trained herself to use via online videos. The machine presented a world of business opportunities, but Harrison decided that Light + Paper would be rooted in hand-cut original designs, which she began to sell as multiples online in 2014.

"I was shocked at how quickly
I became close with people
I met through the maker
scene in Toronto. No one
understands your job better
than another maker."

Each of Harrison's designs begins simply, with a piece of paper, an X-Acto knife, and inspirations that range from botanical to intergalactic. She has carved everything from bicycle ornaments to a wooden stand-up mini model of the Toronto skyline, but Light + Paper is chiefly known for its diaphanous organ collection, which features everything from brains to kidneys. "When I first started, my partner was studying epidemiology and his anatomy books were everywhere," she says. "He said, 'Your patterns are so organic and natural, you should make something from the human body.'" The two settled on the world's most important symbol, a human heart, which houses repeat patterns within its walls.

Light + Paper artworks can take upwards of forty hours to create. "I don't start producing it with a laser cutter until I can do the piece first by hand," she says. "When I first started cutting paper and could create something really nice it was satisfying to think, 'Oh, I'm good at creating something. I can be good at art. I just hadn't tried the art I was good at yet.'"

Ali Harrison | Founder, Maker   131

PRODUCT
Holding Pattern (painting),
Arches (pillow)

MATERIALS
Plaster, paint, brass on
wood panel; 100% linen

Mixed media on wood
panel, 76.2 × 50.8 cm;
screen-printed natural-
linen pillow

Lori
Harrison

Est. 2012

Some might say that life in a big city forces you to find beauty in inconvenient truths, like the permanence of cranes, or even the permanence of decay. One such bright-side enthusiast is Lori Harrison, a fine artist and textile designer who is inspired by the breakdown.

"About ten years ago, I was on a trip with my dad and I saw this old dilapidated clapboard building on the east coast. It was worn and weathered and I got really excited by this idea of beauty and decay," she says. That building, which she photographed and later transformed into a screen print, became the foundation for her self-named line of decorative linen pillows.

Previous to starting her line, Harrison was a trained graphic designer who worked in marketing. "I've always liked three-dimensionality and I loved the idea of creating something two-dimensional—a graphic image—on a three-dimensional form," she says. "That's where I started. I'd like to say I thought it through and had a business plan, but I've been learning as I go."

Almost a decade after starting the line, Harrison still pulls references from her travels. Graffiti walls in Paris, painted sidewalks in Venice Beach, and salt-stained stairs in Montreal are all part of her mindful approach to art, which she defines as encouraging others to

"I remember a mentor of mine said, 'Always look up. Don't look down at your feet.' For me, that means mindfully moving through the world and noticing things."

shift their perspective. "It's all about exploring this idea of beauty in imperfection," she says. "I'm hopefully challenging the people who see or buy my work to see things a little bit differently instead of seeing a graffiti-covered wall as ugly. In the city, we try to control things, but nature is inherently organic and rough. I'm always playing with those two—the tension of right angles versus something more organic and fluid."

That same ethos is reflected in her paintings, which often use left-over scrap linen that she fuses together to create textured surfaces. "I first use ink and let it bleed, and then I layer over top of that very graphic, right-angled shapes," she says. "There's always tension between order and chaos in my work."

Lori Harrison | Designer, Artist   135

Mary Young

It hardly seems plausible that women creating for women is a relatively new norm. But hey, we're here, and thankfully so is Mary Young, a lingerie designer who founded her business with just that goal. "I was never a big fan of lingerie, mostly because I felt very alienated by the advertising," she says. "When I decided to actually study it, I realized there was a big gap in how women were being served, and basically underserved. Many women weren't being spoken to in a positive way." And so, fresh out of Ryerson School of Fashion in 2014, Young began designing a collection that not only embraced natural curves but also sought to liberate women from the confinement of conventional body ideals. "I wanted to make sure women felt confident in what they're wearing, versus trying to reshape their body to try and find confidence," she says.

MARY YOUNG bras feature soft cups, with no padding or under-wire. "The natural shape of a breast is different for everyone—they're rarely perky or perfectly round," she says. Her panties are similarly relaxed, whether they're sexy, multi-strap thongs or minimalist, mesh high-waisters. To ensure max comfort and quality, each of Young's pieces are made using bamboo jerseys, knits, and soft elastics that are sourced locally.

"Seeing women starting to feel empowered through their own decisions and celebrating their bodies is what motivates me to keep going."

Young sees herself at the centre of the maker spectrum, operating a small but mighty design studio out of Toronto, with most of the production completed in Montreal. "I want people to experience the product, whether it's in-store or online, and feel like there's a big company behind it." In reality, however, she says, "Someone had a hand in it every step of the way."

Vibrant hues and curvilinear cutouts are just a few marks of high design, but more than fashion, Young's work is all about body positivity. "The biggest inspiration is the conversations I've had with my customers. I've heard women say, 'I've never purchased lingerie as a gift to myself. It's always been with the thought of someone else,'" she says. "Hearing that women are changing the way they not only see themselves but support themselves . . . it's changing the narrative we've been raised to believe, that there's one type of sexy."

PRODUCT
Emery Bra and Thong in pink

MATERIALS
80% nylon, 20% mesh

Pink bra with a double-layer mesh
cup, single-layer mesh thong

Mary Young | CEO, Designer   139

Matter Company

Est. 2000

Given today's thriving all-natural beauty landscape, it's easy to take for granted our abundance of options. They were certainly far from the norm back in the late 1990s, when Denise Williams began her foray into the magical, healing world of herbal remedies.

The Jamaican-born founder was enrolled in environmental studies at the University of Toronto when a friend living in an off-the-grid community exposed her to the natural powers of plants. "In biology class, I remember being so enchanted with the complexity of the makeup of a flower and how it is life-giving," she says. Inspired, she took a year off to study herbalism and plant therapy alongside a renowned herbalist, before whipping up her own chemical-free salves and first aid ointments in her home kitchen. Williams's initial offerings were inspired by a friend who was pregnant at the time. The pre- and post-natal care products for mothers and holistic, organic skin care products for babies resonated in a then-lacking market, and became the foundation for Matter Company, which Williams launched in 2000.

Over the past two decades, Williams has spun Matter into a vast array of products, all rooted in the therapeutic value of herbs. Each product begins with an herbal-infused oil that is slow-cooked for up to twenty-four hours before it is blended with emollients and

"As a young immigrant child, I felt most comfortable in natural surroundings. I was first introduced to the Canadian wilderness from trips to a friend's cottage in Muskoka and I think this is where I felt my first sense of belonging to this land."

aromatherapy oils. Williams says the benefits can be profound. "For the baby line in particular, the essential oils play a role in helping to develop children's sense of smell," she says. To that end, citrus top notes are crafted to smell sweet and candy-like.

Matter's herbs are culled worldwide, with highlights from Canada's most impressive indigenous plants, such as sumac berries, rose hips, and St. John's wort. Horsetail, for instance, is sourced from B.C. and used in Matter's hand cream. "Horsetail is a prehistoric plant and is really high in silica, which is already in the makeup of our skin and nails," she says.

Matter's outdoor collection includes biodegradable soaps and washes, as well the ever-popular hand creams, salves, and rubs inspired by Williams's love of camping. "If I'm on a hiking trip or canoe trip or a portage and I'm in a forest, I'm looking at what's growing on the ground," she says. "Energetically, plants have a lot going on." The popular All Heal Salve features comfrey, a plant used for its anti-inflammatory healing properties, and chickweed, which soothes itches.

While Williams is credited as one of the city's natural beauty pioneers, she doesn't rest on her laurels. "We were one of the first on the scene, but it's always about staying abreast of what's exciting now," she says. "People are finally 'getting' natural beauty, and that's really exciting."

PRODUCT
Biodegradable Soap (bars), *All Heal Salve* (top tin), *Heat Rub* (bottom tins)

MATERIALS
Herbs, plant-based oils, pure essential oils

Selections from the Outdoors Collection, formulated for protection from the elements

Michelle Ross

Est. 2010

Michelle Ross wants you to wear her jewellery forever. "I've never followed trends," she says. "I'd rather you love the same piece five and ten years from now." Her idiosyncratic, textured pieces often include reworked vintage brass, semiprecious stones, and antique findings that tell a story—one she hopes will be entwined with yours. "They are bold pieces, but they don't wear you, they become part of your wardrobe and self," she says.

Ross has been making jewellery since the age of six, but she didn't pursue it as a career until she was deep in design training, first at NSCAD University in Halifax and later at the London College of Fashion. She'd always envisioned designing womenswear collections with intricate textiles, but upon creating her graduate collection, she subconsciously shifted course. "I noticed that I had started to weave jewellery into so much of the clothing I was making," she says. The collection featured a dress made of Parisian brass chain, freshwater pearls, and semiprecious stones, which prompted a professor to encourage her to launch a jewellery line.

Shortly after Ross's return to Toronto in 2010, she did just that. She has since amassed a following for her distinctive, knitted brass-collar necklaces, hammered brass pendants, and vintage chain-link earrings,

"I didn't want to design something people weren't actually going to use in their daily life. I always wanted to make timeless pieces, whether it was in fashion or jewellery."

all of which are handmade. "People will often say they are more works of art than something they'd go buy at any store," she says.

Ross's love for elaborate textiles still plays a central role in her pieces, which often feature embroidery techniques using freshwater pearls and metallic thread. She usually begins a piece by sourcing materials, then designs around the materials that speak to her, rather than seeking materials for a preconceived piece. "I'll hammer, drill, and really see what they can do," she says. Often, these materials are sourced from Ross's travels to places like India and France, and include anything from brass chain to resin to vintage chandelier parts. "When I'm travelling, I'm often looking at textiles, which is why the majority of my jewellery is very tactile. I want people to touch it."

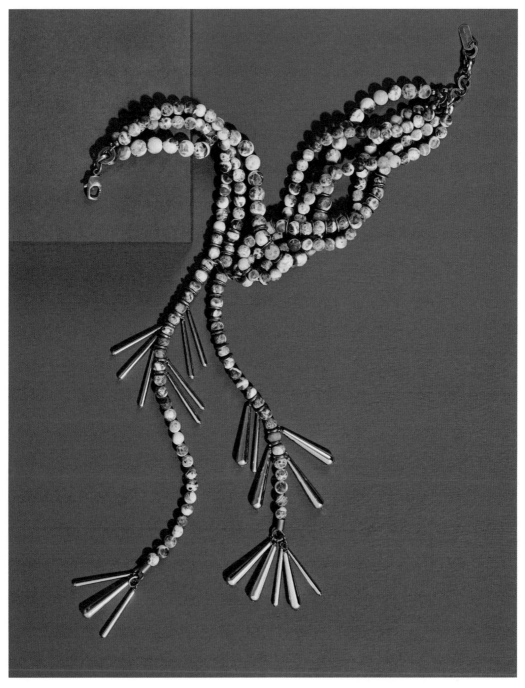

PRODUCT
Ceila Necklace

MATERIALS
Sodalite, brass, rhodium

An asymmetrical frosted sodalite necklace
featuring a silver-fringed drop

Michelle Organ | Founder

Mima Ceramics

Est. 2015

It's certainly a testament to the strength of the maker movement that even at the peak of the digital age, the city is alight with thriving studio spaces built with the express purpose of inspiring creative collaboration.

One such space is The Shop, an open pottery studio for beginners and professional makers alike. "The studio was opened as a space to be able to meet people and see what's going on in the world of pottery and learn from others," says Michelle Organ, The Shop's owner and the creator of Mima Ceramics. "On my end, it's great to see different people come in and how they can take the same lump of clay and make it into whatever they want it to be."

After falling in love with pottery while studying product design at Parsons School of Design in New York, Organ moved back home to Toronto, created a temporary workspace in her parents' basement, and used the kilns of studio artist friends across the city. "There weren't many creative communal spaces at the time," she says. And so, The Shop, a "gym for pottery" as she describes it, was born. The makerspace quickly became a hub for ceramicists to work, learn, and collaborate, on a drop-in or membership basis.

PRODUCT
Clockwise from top left: *Water Carafe atop Lid/Cup,*
Bud Vase, Large Grid Bowl atop Small Grid Bowl,
Bud Vase, Water Carafe with Lid/Cup, Short White Mug

MATERIALS
Stoneware clay   Various handmade ceramics

151

When she's not busy at its helm, Organ is creating her own small-batch, wheel-thrown and slipcast pieces. "My pieces are all functional," she says. "I want people to want to use them on a daily basis, to add a little something special to their daily routine."

And sure, they're functional, but there's something delightfully playful about them too—Organ's brushstrokes dance across mugs, bowls, plates, and planters, which seems fitting given that "Mima" is her childhood nickname. "I've always made things, as a kid and as an adult. I need to use my hands," she says.

"I always say that wheel throwing is ninety percent mental," she says. It's a multi-day, sometimes multi-week process, which lends itself to a bit of chance, since the mould might not always co-operate with the desired shape. After the piece is cast the maker returns a day later to trim, carve, and shape. "You have to be very relaxed," says Organ. The final touches, which include glazing, are when her signature style emerges. "I like the idea of seeing the maker's mark in my pieces. It forces me to be a little easier on myself when I'm being a perfectionist."

"I like to keep things pretty simple but play with pops of colour or pops of design, texture, or shape."

Est. 2017 # Okayok

A pleasant side effect of the social media age is the premium placed on self-expression, something that is central to Okayok, Adrienne Butikofer's quirky fashion line. "My personal style has always been a little offbeat," says the designer. "I think in quips, which often make their way onto my clothes."

After learning how to sew at an early age, Butikofer often made her own outfits, but didn't initially consider it a career. "I actually went into sciences for university, but then I realized I had a point of view and a passion," she says. She enrolled in the fashion program at Fanshawe College and started selling her own wares soon after. A decade, a recession, and a few iterations later, she launched Okayok in 2017. "I finally felt like, through trial and error, I found a brand direction that really worked," she says. Her graphic print T-shirts, colour-block separates, and vibrant accessories, which she describes as "alt-leisure," not only work, they brim with personality.

"My work is about connecting to people's individuality," she says. "I'm never sure how far my ideas will resonate so it's always exciting to see people immediately identify with them. A visceral reaction and an expression of joy is the goal." And for her part, Butikofer relates to many of the slogans that make their way onto Okayok pieces. The Late

"I have a really nice community of other women makers and I feel so much more connected to them than to other fashion designers."

Bloomer sweatshirt, for instance, is a self-effacing reference to her own career. "I'm in my late thirties and I've finally fallen into my natural groove," she laughs.

Part of that groove is the balance between fashion design and the craft of making. "My biggest challenge as a fashion maker has always been time. My goal is always to release seasonal collections according to the fashion calendar, but it almost always gets overtaken by keeping up with the present. My thoughts are at least a year ahead," says Butikofer. "Knowing how to reproduce is a part of being a maker. You're an artist who happens to make one hundred pieces of your art. It's a balance between being a designer and a manufacturer, and doing both well."

PRODUCT
*Confetti Hologram Tee, Pink
Shade Tee, Cloud Sweatshirt*

MATERIALS
Cotton, heat
appliqué vinyl

Hand-cut and -arranged rose-gold vinyl
confetti sweatshirt; graphic tee; sweatshirt
with hand-arranged puffy cloud print

157

(Left to right)
Andy Wilkin | Co-founder **Michelle Wilkin** | Co-owner
Jessie Wilkin | Co-founder **Rob Wilkin** | Co-owner

Pilot Coffee Roasters

Est. 2009

Cold brew in a can is one of those things you would have said "huh?" to a few years ago, but now rolls smoothly off the tongue. The city's coffee landscape has changed drastically in the past decade, and it's thanks largely to Pilot Coffee Roasters, the city's OG indie coffee institution launched by Andy and Jessie Wilkin in 2009.

The couple met in Andy's hometown of Wellington, New Zealand, back in 2002. The local roaster scene was thriving, but had yet to hit Toronto, something the two vowed to make happen upon their return. "Torontonians like to support local businesses. We wanted to take a risk and bring a new concept to Toronto," says Jessie.

And so in 2009 they did, opening a small roastery and café on Queen East, which they quickly outgrew. A few years later, Andy's brother and sister-in-law, Rob and Michelle, moved from New Zealand to join the now family-run business, and Pilot unveiled what would become its flagship location: a former warehouse space fitted with a roastery, tasting bar, and training lab. The large-scale East End location is where Pilot's beans are roasted and its cold brew production works are housed. "The facility is large but accessible, so you can have a truly artisanal experience," says Jessie. "The tasting bar is a unique experience. You can try things like coffee cocktails and different brewing methods, and learn the story of how we source and make the coffee."

PRODUCT
Pilot Cold Brew (latte and black)

MATERIALS
Coffee, water or organic milk, nitrogen

A precisely measured
single serving

Pilot's approach is rooted in quality, which Andy ensures at the get-go by travelling the world to find the best beans. Recent sourcing missions have taken him to Costa Rica, Brazil, Kenya, and Ethiopia. "We've worked with a lot of the same farmers for over five years now. It's all about supporting each other," he says. "We want to make their coffee and their lives better. We do that by paying them premium prices, visiting them, and working with them to challenge them to improve their quality and take different steps to make sure they're doing everything responsibly—from looking after their pickers, to being innovative with how they're planning and choosing the varieties of coffee."

"We've spent a lot of resources on constantly innovating. It has an impact on the greater coffee community because it pushes everyone forward."

Jessie Wilkin

PRODUCT
Clockwise from top: *Sex Oil, Nourishing +*
Revitalizing Moisturizer, Regenerating +
Stimulating Exfoliator, Radiant Body Oil,
Rejuvenating + Hydrating Face Serum

MATERIALS
Organic plant ingredients

Holistic skin and body
products for all skin types

Province
Apothecary

Est. 2012

Some say it's lonely at the top, but that couldn't be further from the truth for Julie Clark, a natural beauty trailblazer who thrives in the comfort of her fellow go-getters. "I'm blown away by how many amazing entrepreneurial women there are in Toronto," she says. "I have a lot of friends who are just kicking ass—it's so inspiring." Her brand, Province Apothecary, is one that resonates in the oft-crowded world of natural beauty. But it wasn't always like that. "When I started in 2012, natural beauty was still pretty niche," she says. Fast-forward seven years and a few store relocations, and Clark's small-batch, plant-based skin care products reign supreme.

Clark's own experience with eczema and asthma was what led her down the path of natural beauty. "I'd always been on steroids and lots of really terrible things to try and heal my body, and I hit a breaking point," she says. Determined to find a natural solution, she quit her career in costume design in New York, moved to Toronto, and studied aromatherapy, aesthetics, and herbalism. "The experience changed my life," she says.

Not only did she find her own cure, she discovered a love for giving facials and began offering them out of her home using her own homemade products. "I wasn't happy with the quality I was seeing in the market at the time," she says. "As an aromatherapist, I learned so much

"It's so awesome to see natural
and green beauty really thrive
and be successful and change...
even my mom uses it."

about essential oils, which all stem from plant medicine." One of the brand's first products was an eczema balm that took Clark three years to develop. "It took lots of research, studying medical journals, learning herbal medicine and understanding what works together before I found the perfect formula."

As the name suggests, Province Apothecary features ingredients from across Canada, from Nova Scotia seaweed to Ontario lavender to Alberta beeswax. "I do lots of research and connect with small, sustainable producers and farmers," she says. Those ingredients sit alongside globally sourced ones, such as rosehip from Bulgaria. "I'm so lucky that I work with amazing farmers, producers, herbalists, and botanists who I trust, and who produce the best-quality ingredients in the most sustainable way."

Almost a decade after offering them out of her own home, treatments are still the backbone of the business. "I fell in love with helping people with their skin issues," says Clark. "Our treatment space is where I feel a lot of the magic happens, and where I get to do tons of experimentation and try new things." The brand's treatment space is just down the block from its flagship store, but soon the experience will be offered internationally. "My goal is always to empower all our clients to take care of their skin 365 days a year," she says.

Julie Clark | Founder   167

Devin Schaffner | Co-founder, Lead Designer
Natalie Schaffner | Co-founder, Director of Operations
Fitz Schaffner | Daughter

Est. 2014   # Rekindle

In these social media–saturated times, one thing we can all get behind is makers with the motivation to bring people together IRL. "The most important thing in life is building relationships with people," says Devin Schaffner of Rekindle, an industrial design company he founded with his partner, Natalie, to do just that. "We aim to build those connections through our products."

Schaffner's background as an interior designer informs his holistic approach. "I was really interested in the products I was placing into the spaces I was working on and the idea of designing them," he says. "I thought, 'That's actually a job!'" So he went back to school to study industrial design at OCAD University, where he created Rekindle as a thesis project.

"My motives stemmed from the disposable society we're living in," he says. "I really wanted to create things people would have around for a long time, and the only way to do that is to distill it down to what makes us most connected to those things—it's typically having an emotional or sentimental attachment to the connections you forged while using them." Rekindle's wooden, ceramic, leather, and brass accessories and small furnishings—like its stackable round plates, or the multifunctional side table that can also be used as a stool or a serving tray—are

"I learn and figure things out by actually doing. I'm a learner through doing. Maker makes sense to me. It's how my mind works."

all rooted in age-old traditions. "When I'm designing," says Schaffner, "I think about what we've been doing for a very long time that's not going away: sharing a beer with friends, playing games at home, or sitting around candlelight."

Aging gracefully is another of Rekindle's design tenets. "Material selections are so important to the way something looks over time," he says. To wit, Schaffner uses only locally sourced, domestic wood species such as walnut and white oak. "There are lots of options around the world but if you have something right outside your back door, you should use it."

Schaffner works out of a woodworking co-op, which he shares with eight other small businesses. "It's a great environment to be a part of and I'm constantly reaching out to other craftspeople to see how we can collaborate with each other and help each other's businesses grow," he says. Connection seems baked into Rekindle's every step.

PRODUCT
Clockwise from top left: *Offset Tealight Holder Small,*
Brasstix, Offset Tealight Holder Multi 3, All Plate Large
(with Brasstix), All Plate Medium, Fika Tray

MATERIALS
Solid white oak,
walnut

Selections from the
On the Table collection

PRODUCT
Vita Da Sogno

MATERIALS
Canson Baryta
photographique paper

Museum-quality,
archival fine art giclée,
limited edition of 99,
109.2 × 76.2 cm (5 cm trim)

Samara Shuter

Est. 2012

"I don't think I'd ever be capable of doing just one genre," says Samara Shuter, a Toronto fine artist known for her vibrant large-scale paintings of men's suits. "There are so many things I want to try and so many mediums I'm curious about!" Her curiosity is apparent when you see the multidimensional nature of Shuter's art: It's abstract, yet figurative. It's imposing, yet playful. It's decidedly modern, while firmly rooted in sartorial classics.

Shuter's fascination with menswear began early, when she'd sketch bow ties as a child with her father, a textile businessman with a proclivity for ties. "We worked out from the bow tie to the lapel and I'd make shoulders," she says. "My father would say, 'It's starting to look like a person.' I was never concerned with the face." It was all about patterns, something she'd reignite a passion for years later while pursuing a career in film circa 2012.

"I was on a snowboarding trip with my now wife and she bought a jacket with a tag that had the most incredible palette of colours," she says. The tag inspired an abstract painting. "I was going through old memory boxes and found all of these doodles of suits I had done during elementary school," she says. "And for some reason after I found them, I looked at the abstract painting and thought, 'There's more to this.'"

"What I enjoy most is the interactive element of experiencing my work with others. Meeting people from all walks of life and learning what speaks to them."

So she drew a line drawing overtop the abstract and it became her first work. Positive feedback—and her first sale, to a collector in Florida—was immediate. Now Shuter paints full-time and takes advantage of the reach of social media to sell her work across the country and around the world, though mostly into the U.S.

"Everyone asks why I don't paint a woman in a suit" she says, "and it's not that I don't want to, but what attracted me to menswear was how structured and symmetric it is. Women are often more curvaceous." Symmetry plays a big part in her paintings of musical instruments as well, but there's still plenty of movement in her work. Most paintings begin with Shuter photographing friends walking and jumping in stylish get-ups. "I have one buddy who always breaks a sweat," she laughs. "We'll go shoot in a condo or the park and he'll jump off a small ledge a hundred times until I get that great air shot."

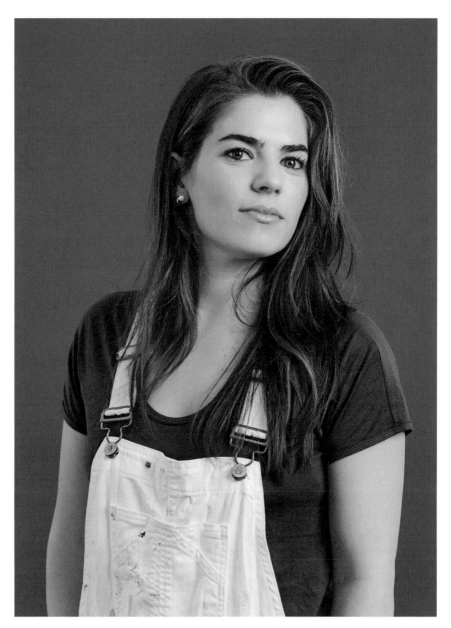

Samara Shuter | Creative Director, Fine Artist   175

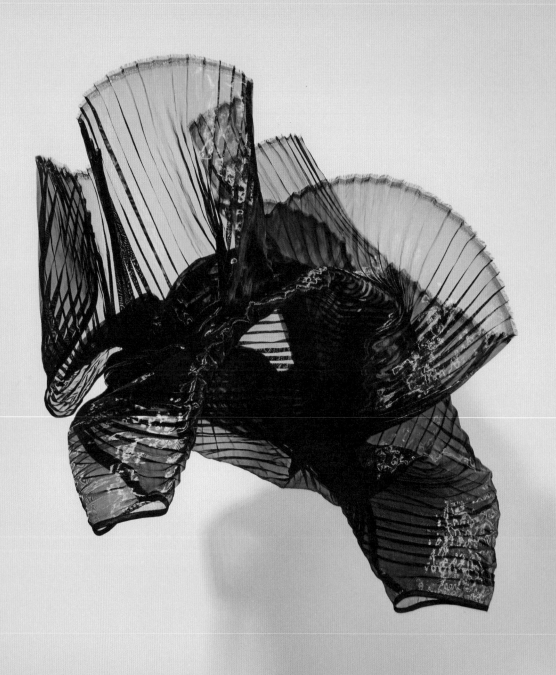

PRODUCT
C.SS109PN

MATERIALS
Nylon

Wrapped blouse created
from a single piece of pleated
and folded nylon

Sid Neigum

Est. 2011

In the often sparse landscape of Canadian high fashion, Sid Neigum's rise to the top has been a particularly patriotic bright spot. The designer has achieved critical mass on an international circuit for his meticulous, sculptural womenswear. But despite the acclaim, his craft (and business) remains firmly planted in the city that gave him wings.

Growing up in conservative, oil-rich Drayton Valley, Alberta, Neigum's only exposure to fashion was through his grandmother, a seamstress who made clothes for him and his sister without the use of patterns. "It was the first time I saw somebody transform fabric into garments," he says. Despite his growing interest in design over the years, he first pursued a math and science major. "I didn't even know there was such a thing as a designer," he says. He soon figured it out, and in 2010 enrolled at the Fashion Institute of Technology in New York. By 2012, he was showing his collections on runways in Toronto, where he racked up countless awards and accolades in the ensuing years.

His math and science skills were never left too far behind—Neigum's collections often include references to ideas he first encountered during his undergrad. The famous Golden Ratio, for example, appears frequently, taking form as everything from an oversized fit to

"I started creating things I wanted to wear. As it turned into a business, I kept my DNA but thought so much more about what other people wanted to wear."

a cropped length to an extra long sleeve. Once, he melded over six hundred pieces of laser-cut, modular origami into statement vests, dresses, and coats.

Lately, Neigum's approach has become much more refined, and while those equations are less overtly visible, they are baked into each of his often airy, ethereal designs. "As things progressed and as I learned, I started being able to use lighter and softer fabrics," he says. "Being able to expand on that to other new fabrics was part of the learning process."

For years, Neigum has held court at the Toronto Fashion Incubator, where he works alongside a team of seamstresses to produce each collection in between his busy runway schedule and sales travel to New York, London, and beyond. "It's nice to come home, hibernate, and work," he says.

And while he likes staying tucked away, it's fair to say that fashion is embedded in his everyday life. His girlfriend, Beaufille designer Chloé Gordon, is his unofficial partner and fit-model. "I think design is ninety percent of what we're talking about every night," he says.

Sid Neigum | Designer   179

Hoda Paripoush | Founder, Creative Director

Sloane Tea

Est. 2011

Teatime is a universally pleasant time of day, but for Hoda Paripoush, it's much more than that. The Sloane Tea founder was born in India after her family escaped the increasing persecution of Bahá'ís in Iran at the outset of the revolution. After a decade in India they came to Canada as religious refugees, and eventually settled in Brockville, Ontario, a small town with little diversity. "Tea was the one ritual we had no matter the uncertainty or chaos surrounding us," she says.

Paripoush initially pursued a career in naturopathic medicine, but she kept coming back to her favourite pastime. "There was something about it that calmed me and I remember having an epiphany and thinking, 'If I could do anything in the world, I'd do something with tea.'" So, listening to her calling, she enrolled in classes and became the first tea sommelier accredited in both Canada and the U.S.

But there was still more: "It was kind of like being a chef and having read the best cookbooks in the world but never having been in the kitchen," she says. So, she decided to source the ingredients herself, visiting tea farms in China, Japan, and beyond. Today, those travels are central to Sloane's precision. Take, for instance, its Earl Grey, which features black tea from Assam, India, as well as cold-pressed Sicilian bergamot. "I tested over eighty-three types of bergamot before I found

"Without even knowing it, tea was in my blood. I was never asked, 'Did you have water today?' It was, 'Did you drink tea today?'"

this one," she says. "I wanted a bergamot flavour that was as true to the smell of opening up the fruit as possible."

Despite Sloane's small size, Paripoush's travels have allowed her to form close relationships with the farmers she sources directly from. "Normally tea goes from the garden to an auction to a broker, exporter, importer, distributor, then to retailers, which takes anywhere from nine months to a year," she says. Sloane's teas arrive within three months of harvest, allowing for a higher absorption rate when blended. Once they arrive, they are layered in small batches and left to blend for as long as two days. "We really try to honour the farmers and the quality of what they worked so incredibly hard to produce," says Paripoush. "When we're blending, we're blending for quality first. Cost, for better or worse, is the last thing we think about."

PRODUCT
Left: *Rouge Provence, Tropical Green;*
centre, from top: *Marakesh Mint, Ginger Twist,*
Mint Chocolate, Masala Chai Classic;
right, from top: *Earl Grey Classic, Citron Calm*

MATERIALS
Tea (*Camellia sinensis*),
spices, fruits, florals

Whole-leaf organic teas and
ingredients sourced directly
from origin, blended and
packaged locally

Katie Wilson (left),
Kyle Wilson | Owners, Chocolate Makers

Soul Chocolate

Est. 2015

Travel has inspired many a maker, and in the cases of Katie and Kyle Wilson, it helped them build a viable business out of an intense, life-long love of chocolate. "Katie once bit her friend because she stole her last piece of chocolate," says Kyle, who founded Soul Chocolate along-side his now wife in 2015.

The couple met through mutual connections almost a decade ago, and throughout their courtship, frequently travelled off the beaten path. A few years ago they came across a part café, part chocolate lab in Wellington, New Zealand, that offered over thirty types of chocolate. "Previous to this trip, I didn't think making chocolate could be a career," says Katie. "It really got me thinking about what chocolate is and how it is made."

The wheels were turning. Back in Toronto, Katie enrolled in the chocolatier program at George Brown College and started experiment-ing out of the couple's second bedroom. "Making my first bar from scratch was so gratifying," she says. "It inspired me to continue learn-ing and experimenting. I wanted to make really good chocolate more accessible, and show people how complex chocolate can be."

Meanwhile, Kyle began rebuilding vintage espresso machines and working in various cafés before the couple opened theirs. "I spent five

"I like being able to infinitely tweak something to make it better or different. It doesn't always have to be exactly the same. You're celebrating the uniqueness." **Kyle Wilson**

or six years learning about coffee," he says. "The production process mirrors cacao almost identically." The two used Kyle's specialty coffee skills to develop its small-batch dark chocolate recipes, all of which are rooted in the special properties of the different varieties of cacao.

Their Madagascar 60 percent dark chocolate, for example, features caramelized milk powder to add a rich, malty flavour to the cacao's natural fruitiness. "Madagascar chocolate piques both of our interests," says Kyle. "It's so unique. It didn't taste at all like what I expected dark chocolate to be." The uniqueness extends to its labels, which are so delightfully hard to miss in all their kaleidoscopic glory.

As the Wilsons expand, they are hoping to source directly from their favourite destinations in Africa, South America, and beyond, and build relationships that enrich both sides—and not just monetarily. "A lot of the farmers have never tasted what they're producing," says Kyle. Their goal is to create 100 percent direct trade with those farmers for their cacao, elevating prices and quality for all. "There are people along the whole process who are spending countless hours to grow something and getting paid very little. We're trying to highlight that a little more and pay as much as we can and shift that mindset behind chocolate from a candy that costs a buck to something that's specialty and is worth more."

PRODUCT
From top: *Venezuela 50% Tea with Milk, Ecuador*
75% Dark Chocolate, Guatemala 68% Dark Chocolate,
Venezuela 75% Dark Chocolate, Dominican Republic 70%
Dark Chocolate, Papua New Guinea 77% Dark Chocolate

MATERIALS
Cacao, organic
cane sugar

Single-origin chocolate
made from raw ingredients,
sourced ethically and direct
from the farm

187

Est. 2017 # Spare Label

In an age of constant digital stimulation, the art of letting go is just that: an art. It's also something Sabine Spare has made an essential part of the process behind her line of clothing and accessories, Spare Label. The Belleville-born designer was working in costume construction when she happened upon marbling, an ancient surface technique (seriously, its roots can be traced back as far as 986 CE) while doing a workshop in New York. "I found it so beautiful and meditative," she says.

Today, she incorporates the technique into each of her pieces: hand-marbled dresses, tote bags, backpacks, and the like. While Spare works with silks, cottons, and leathers, each piece is a monotype, meaning no two pieces ever look quite alike. Her patterns often resemble water and stone. "I love that I can make certain decisions, such as the colours or the patterning technique that I use, but ultimately the fluid dynamics influence how the image appears," she says.

Spare is a maker in every sense of the word, but she doesn't shy away from the potential of technology to permanently alter her field. "I would define a maker as anyone who enjoys rolling up their sleeves and getting their hands dirty," she says. "But that doesn't mean they can't have technological assistance." To wit, Spare has collaborated with robotics architect Joey Jacobson on The Aqueous Project, an ongoing

"I don't ever just want
to be sitting behind a
desk, removed from my
collaborators and clients."

exploration into the automation of marbling. Because of environmental influences on the materials, even a machine-operated process can produce a one-of-a-kind result. "It's partly industrial innovation and partly conceptual exploration because it asks the question, does a maker need to be directly involved to be making?"

That's an interesting question to be asking, given that Spare is so connected to her pieces that she can spot energetic differences between them. "I work with studio assistants on my large-scale marbling, and our conversation and their presence affect the work. I like to think about how that manifests itself in the patterning," she says. "It's so subtle and it's not something that would be immediately evident, but I can notice the difference in a pattern that I've made with one person from the ones I've made with another."

PRODUCT
Aril Tunic

MATERIALS
20% silk, 80% cotton

A hand-printed tunic,
cut from a monotype textile

PRODUCT
Spirit of York Vodka (left), *Spirit of York Gin*

MATERIALS
Ontario-sourced ingredients

Premium vodka distilled to its
purest form; gin featuring the
essence of 15 selected botanicals

Spirit of York

Est. 2017

In the century and a half since Toronto's Gooderham and Worts
was considered the largest distillery in Canada, its former home,
the Distillery District, has gone from defunct 'hood to movie set
to revitalized retail and residential goldmine. And in all that time,
somehow no one thought to open a new distillery in the historic
neighbourhood until 2017 and the launch of Spirit of York, a premium
spirits distillery rooted in the old world.

Spirit of York is in part the brainchild of Germain Guitor, who left a
prominent career in the food and beverage industry to try his hand at
the world of craft spirits alongside business partner Brent Peters. "It
was an opportunity for us to own something and to be able to pull in all
the various labours that were required to make this a success," he says.
He wasn't alone—Spirit of York is a passion project for many, including
lead distiller Mark Harrop, Maryke Ballard, Simon Ho, and a group of
local entrepreneurs led by Robert Cudney and Sean Roosen. "Our team
is an eclectic group—each individual brings their own skill set to the
table. Together we made our vision a reality, and are proud to offer the
world distinctive, premium spirits."

Spirit of York is certainly distinct, beginning with its spring
water sourced in the aptly named Springwater, Ontario. Using

"Our whole idea is we want to celebrate the social cultural fabric of what makes this city great."

hand-assembled German equipment, 100 percent Ontario rye is distilled just once, as opposed to the standard three or four times. "Somehow through the years, multiple distilling has come to equal smoothness and that's not necessarily true," says Guitor. "We distill it once in order to make sure we retain that beautiful taste within our product." Its gin features fifteen botanicals selected by the master distiller, which macerate for eighteen hours to create a balanced and refreshing gin.

All of this is done behind floor-to-ceiling glass at Spirit of York's exquisite reclaimed facility, where visitors can watch the magic happen and sample the end result. "The idea is that we want to be very transparent about what we do," says Guitor. "Everything is made with local ingredients by local folks with local passions."

(Left to right)

Maryke Ballard | Marketing and Events Manager   **Germain Guitor** | Founder

Mark Harrop | Director of Operations   **Simon Ho** | Director of Sales   195

Talia Silva

Est. 2013

If the essence of "maker" could be embodied in a single person, it'd likely be Talia Silva. The ceramicist is soft-spoken and contemplative, and approaches her work with a perfectionism that ensures the reverence that follows it around town. "My work is about capturing a feeling," she says.

Silva is known for her delicate lampshades, playful vases, and vintage-inspired bottle forms. "When I first started, I was interested in the translucency of porcelain, to incorporate light," she says. Much of Silva's work is inspired by our experience within the natural world—coastal landscapes, mountainscapes, and sunlight all play into her work. "So much is happening behind the scenes that we can't necessarily see," she says. "It's all very meditative." However, Silva insists the translation isn't a literal one. "I'm drawn to the interplay of light and shadow—how sunlight is captured by the ridges and creases and layers, casting shadows and illuminating different sections, and how that changes as the sun passes through," she says. "To me, natural landscapes are a reflection of emotional/internal landscapes."

Silva discovered ceramics while studying environmental design at OCAD University, but didn't embrace it full-time until relatively recently. While working as a designer at an Italian interiors firm, she

"A lot of people say my
work is very meditative.
It's deceptively simple."

honed her pottery skills on the side as part of an all-female, mixed discipline studio. It led to her first exhibition in 2013, at an all-female design show, where her work caught the eye of shops and clients alike.

Most of Silva's pieces are slipcast, which is the technique of pouring liquid clay into a plaster mould, where it forms a layer on the wall of the mould. Hand-carved details are added later, which Silva says are the result of intuitive mark-making and deep contemplation. "A lot of those ideas came from playing around in the studio and allowing that time to see what's possible," she says. "A lot of good things happen and a lot of not-so-good things happen. I might have an object for a year or two or three before it's something."

PRODUCT
Carved Porcelain Vase and Bottles

MATERIALS
Porcelain, transparent glaze

Slipcast ceramics made of white
porcelain, individually hand-carved

PRODUCT
The Breezy Scarf

MATERIALS
Natural fibres, botanical
inks and dyes

A lightweight scarf hand-printed
and hand-dyed with plant-based
inks and dyes

Tania Love

Est. 2012

For most of us, it requires great effort to be at one with nature. But it's always been easy for Tania Love, a multidisciplinary artist who imbues her work with elements of the outdoors. "A lot of my time was spent in the trees, picking cherries, and being around things that were growing," she says of her childhood in Grimsby, Ontario. "That naturally informed a feeling for working with my hands and being engaged with the environment."

Love's art includes drawing and installation, and also extends beyond the canvas to wearable textiles, which she makes using small-batch methods. "For me, this kind of practice opens conversations with the people who experience my work," she says. "It's finding that bridge between the natural world and our cultural lives." Multiple steps, which include preparing the fibres with mordants, screen-printing, dyeing, washing, and pressing, are all done by hand, which she says is essential to the craft. "In doing work that is very time-intensive, I'm engaging in our life cycle—there's a process of time," she says. "When I'm working with plant materials, it's a way of connecting to changes in seasons and time."

She sketches her designs and renders them onto a screen for printing, but the initial ideas are plucked directly from nature, as are her

"I try to get out to Toronto's parks regularly and find those moments of the beauty of nature within the urban context. Even looking at the cracks in the pavement is an expression of nature to me."

inks and dyes, which are created with everything from pomegranate rind to sumac leaves to black walnut she sources on walks around the Niagara escarpment. "When I harvest sumac leaves earlier in the season versus later, or from one year to the next, the colour composition is different because of the growth cycle of the plant," she says. "That's a subtext in my work, the sense that the seasons change and with them nature changes." One of her most popular designs is an anemone print inspired by her parents' garden.

"It points back to that sense of the tactile, to slower rhythms and our relationship with the natural environment," she says. "Our lives are busy, engaged in technology, and we kind of get removed from the natural cycles, like our feeling for the seasons. I want to bring that tactile information and healing from nature back into people's lives by way of something they can wear."

PRODUCT
Natural Croissant

MATERIALS
Flour, butter, milk

Handmade over three days, with
a crispy, flaky exterior and a soft,
custardy interior

Est. 2011

Tasso Baking

If a flaky, buttery croissant that takes three days to make sounds like something you'd definitely like to eat, look no further than Tasso Baking—but you'd better be an early riser. You see, Mike and Olyana Tasso serve up pillowy goodness from their pocket Parliament Street bakeshop exclusively on Friday, Saturday, and Sunday mornings, and they usually sell out well before the brunch crowds start lining the sidewalks. "A croissant has to be sold within a few hours of baking, or it's not the same," says Olyana. "It's a morning pastry. A place that sells croissants after three or four o'clock in the afternoon doesn't make sense to me!"

The couple's baking process includes one day for making the base dough, another for lamination (creating butter-dough layers), and yet another for proofing and baking. You might be shocked by such an old-school approach in the age of automation, but the Tassos wouldn't have it any other way. "We treat it as hours of being together, doing something we really enjoy," says Mike. "There are easier ways to make a living than waking up at three in the morning every Friday, Saturday, and Sunday. But we love it."

The duo stumbled across their signature organically. "Olyana was a fanatic home baker and we thought opening a coffee shop would be

> "We're wholly dedicated to the quality of our pastry—that's what our customers respond to."
>
> **Mike Tasso**

fun," says Mike. "It was typical—we were in our thirties and tired of our jobs at the time." Olyana was always passionate about croissants, but she whipped up everything from muffins to scones, assuming that their customers wanted variety. But it was the croissant that people came back for time and time again. "We went croissant-only in 2015 and we've been rockin' and rollin' ever since," says Mike.

The recipe itself is unique, but rooted in tradition. Olyana describes it as an "evolution of trying many recipes over the years." Each weekend, it morphs into a variety of styles, ranging from pain au chocolat to kouign-amann to cinnamon rolls and back again, to the delight of Tasso's many loyal fans.

The couple runs an intentionally small but mighty ship. "Everyone always says, 'Expansion, expansion, expansion!' But it's more about how much we really love baking, and ensuring consistent quality each bake," says Olyana. "I want to be involved in every step of the process."

Mike Tasso (left), **Olyana Tasso** | Owners, Bakers   207

Victory Patterns

Est. 2010

They say no (wo)man is an island, and in the world of makers that statement rings especially true. Take, for instance, Kristiann Boos, a fashion instructor turned pattern designer whose business model is rooted in fostering creativity in others.

On a trip home from working in London, England, with Topshop and Selfridges, Boos came across a sewing studio in Parkdale that spurred her on a journey into the world of DIY. "I was so intrigued because at the time, sewing was not really a thing people did as a hobby," she says. It was the late 2000s, the peak of the fast-fashion frenzy, when consumers had become largely disassociated from the makers behind their clothes. Tides were shifting, though. "I think things like *Project Runway* started making what goes into making clothes more transparent," says Boos. "People became fascinated with seeing the design process after years of just assuming everything was machine made."

Not only did they want to see, they wanted to *do*: the slow-fashion scene was on the rise. Boos moved home, started teaching at the studio, and brainstormed ways to stitch together a career from sewing. "I wasn't interested in designing my own line and having to tell people to buy something new each season," she says. "Instead, teaching opened up a door for me to see a business model that could be viable—communicating with people who want to sew for themselves."

"All I really care about is
being creative for myself and
fostering that in other people."

And so, Victory Patterns, a modernized guide to sewing, was born. Marrying feminine, minimal, and vintage design elements, Boos dreams up patterns that makers use to create their own one-of-a-kind wardrobes. Available in both print and PDF formats, the patterns come complete with beginner-friendly step-by-step instructions. "I'm passionate about understanding the process of making and I wanted to create a product that puts those answers in there," she says. "I knew from a teaching perspective the questions people would ask."

While each of the patterns comes with suggested fabrications, they're left open for interpretation. "It's so interesting to see what people do with them," says Boos. "I have an idea in mind, and then I see a completely different version than what I thought possible. That's the beauty of it!"

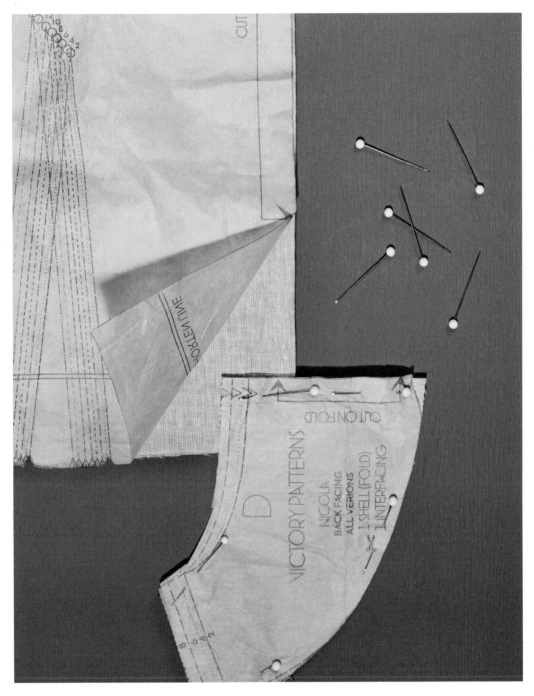

PRODUCT
Nicola Dress

MATERIALS
Tissue paper

CALMING
HAND & BODY
LOTION

HYSSOP + ROSE GERANIUM

100% NATURAL

100% NATUREL CALMANT LOTION MAINS ET CORPS
8 FL OZ / 236 mL

WIII

01

NATURAL DEODORANT SPRAY
BERGAMOT + ELEMI

100% NATURAL OILS
FAIT À 100% D'HUILES NATURELLES

130 ML / 4.4 FL OZ

WIII

02

NATURAL DEODORANT
TEA TREE + PUMPKIN SEED

100% NATURAL OIL
FAIT À 100% D'HUILES NATURELLES

75 G / 2.65 OZ

WIII

03

ROSEMARY

TEA TREE

100 % NATURAL

PURE
PERFUME
OIL

TEA ROOM

PRODUCT
Clockwise from top left: *Calming Hand & Body Lotion, 01 Natural Deodorant Spray, Muscle Soak Bath Salt, 02 Natural Deodorant, Tea Tree Essential Oil, Rosemary Essential Oil, 03 Soothe and Cool, Tea Room Perfume Oil*

MATERIALS
100% pure-grade essential oils

Essential-oil face, body, and active care

Way of Will

Est. 2015

As anyone new to the world of natural beauty has likely bemoaned, finding fitness-related products that are as high-performance as the conventional stuff is an arduous, sweaty matter of trial and error. Remedying that was the impetus behind Way of Will, an active body care brand that harnesses the power of essential oils.

Willie Tsang has always been a scent enthusiast, but he didn't see its potential until he spent months caring for his ailing father. "He had leukemia and the cancer cells spread to his brain. He was confused, but the only time he was awake or got excited was when he smelled scents that were familiar to him," he says. Tsang was inspired. As an avid gym-goer who helmed a successful ceramics business, he knew he could use a hand. So, he recruited his aromatherapist friend Jean Liao and the two put their heads together.

In 2016, they launched Way of Will as a fulsome line of fitness essentials, which included deodorant, body oil, and face oil. "Because of my previous experience, I learned that it's not easy to make it in the market if you only have one or two products," he says. "When you try to tell the story to retailers and customers, they have to have some sort of variety to choose from." He was right: the brand is currently stocked in over three hundred retailers worldwide. Variety remains a point of

"Toronto has a lot of talented designers and makers and I think people are also very supportive. The community feels small but big at the same time."

distinction for Way of Will, which has expanded into various collections of skin care products and wellness giftables, all made in small batches at the brand's Etobicoke facility.

Each product begins with a scent story that not only pleases the senses, but also provides stimulation to the brain and olfactory system. For instance, grapefruit and pine are blended to cleanse and reduce nerve exhaustion in an energizing body wash, while geranium and patchouli are combined in a dry-skin facial toner. In the case of its popular deodorant, essential oils prevent bacteria growth, rather than simply masking odours.

Tsang and Liao obsessively research the functions and interactions of each ingredient before testing their formulations for as long as six months. "A lot of it has to do with our data—everything from analytics to personal preference plays a part," says Tsang. "Seeing people use our products and the reviews on the website really get us going."

Wildcraft

By now, you've likely been inundated with plaques and Pinterest-ready prints emblazoned with the familiar adage "Health is Wealth." And while it's certainly true, so is the inverse—the world of wellness can often feel unattainable to those without endless funds to drop on pricey serums and cleanses. Enter Wildcraft, the accessible alternative, which offers luxurious and affordable natural skin care for the everyday beauty routine.

"My goal is to bring truly natural products to the mainstream," says Laura Whitaker, who founded Wildcraft in 2014. "I really felt there was a gap in the market for skin care that's natural, handmade, and beautifully packaged, but also approachable, and I want to inspire more people to make the switch."

As a young child, Whitaker was inspired by the hands-on creativity of her single mother, who ensured they lived well with their modest resources. When she realized the same principles—living simply, within your means, while still prioritizing health—could be applied to self-care products, it was the catalyst that led to the creation of Wildcraft. "Skin care doesn't need to be complicated or costly in order to be something that's beautiful and performs well," she says.

"It'd be hard to imagine starting our company elsewhere. We got our start because there are so many retailers in Toronto that support companies like ours."

This emphasis on mindfulness and minimalism inspired her first experiments making salves, serums, and creams in her kitchen, and continues to permeate everything Wildcraft does. Simplicity is baked into the brand, reflected in the products, the packaging, and even the marketing. "I don't use extravagant ingredients, make unbelievable claims, or try to create a feeling of unattainability," she says. "That's become the norm in both the conventional and natural beauty industries. A minimalist and unpretentious outlook is part of what sets the brand apart."

That honest approach resonates with a growing audience. Wildcraft grew slowly at first, focusing on indie retailers and pop-up markets in Toronto, but is now carried by more than eighty retailers across the country, and is quickly building a complete collection of personal care products for a variety of skin types and uses. Despite the rapid growth, Wildcraft will always be a small-batch, handmade operation. "There's an authenticity to it," says Whitaker. "Skin care is so intimate, and my customers like to know that what they put on their skin is made by a real person."

PRODUCT
Clockwise from top: *Bergamot Rose Face Cream, Geranium Orange Blossom Face Cream, All-Purpose Salve, Buff Face and Body Scrub, Soak Herbal Bath Blend* (scattered herbs and flowers), *Geranium Orange Blossom Face Cream*

MATERIALS
Organic oils, butters, clays, herbs, flowers, beeswax

All-natural skin care products handmade in small batches

Laura Whitaker | Founder   219

Randi Bergman

Randi Bergman is a writer, editor, podcaster, and consultant who covers a variety of topics, including fashion, art, culture, and lifestyle—sometimes self-deprecatingly, other times seriously. Her work can be seen in the *Globe and Mail*, *The Cut*, *Canadian Art*, *S/ Style*, and *Toronto Life*. Previously she was the executive digital editor at *FASHION Magazine*.

Special thanks to Andrea Bergman, Anne T. Donahue, Erin Dunlop, Tamar Frank, and Suzanne Mandarino.

Cataloguing data is available from Library and Archives Canada
ISBN 978-1-77327-052-4 (hbk.)

Design by Jessica Sullivan

All photography by Saty + Pratha, except pages i, ii, v, 20, 26–27, 66–67, 102, 150–151, 160–161 by Joseph Saraceno and pages 127, 135, 215 by Suech and Beck
Still-life styling by Wilson Wong
Wardrobe styling by Vanessa Taylor and Ingrie Williams
Hair and makeup by Andrew Ly and Robson Oliveira
Creative direction and production by Makejoy.co: Gloria Cheung, Amy Czettisch, and Jill Redden

Editing by Michael Leyne
Proofreading by Renate Preuss

Front cover: Coolican & Company white-oak chair; *endpapers*: Spare Label marble-print tunic; *back cover*: Mima Ceramics carafes with lids/cups

Portrait props by 18 Waits (clothing, p. 1), Attic Gold (jewellery, p. 12), Biko (jewellery, pp. 24, 220), Coolican & Company (stools, pp. 4, 11, 12, 38, 44, 59, 90, 140, 158, 199, 219), Coup de Tête (hats, pp. 1, 44), Dean Davidson (necklace, p. 11; earrings, p. 98), Fitzy (belt, p. 131), Hollis + Morris (stools, pp. 33, 113, 207), Michelle Ross (bracelets, pp. 11, 108; earrings, pp. 120, 144, 180; necklace, p. 144), Okayok (sweatshirt, p. 154), Spare Label (dress, p. 188), and Tania Love (scarf, p. 203).

Printed and bound in China by C&C Offset Printing Co., Ltd.
Distributed in the U.S. by Publishers Group West

Figure 1 Publishing Inc.
Vancouver BC Canada
www.figure1publishing.com